Fun-to-Learn
Bible Lessons:
K–3, Volume 1

Edited by Susan L. Lingo

Loveland, Colorado

Fun-to-Learn Bible Lessons: K–3, Volume 1
Copyright © 1994 Group Publishing, Inc.

Scriptures quoted from **The Youth Bible, New Century Version,** copyright © 1991 by Word Publishing, Dallas, Texas 75039. Used by permission.

Contributors: Nanette Goings, Sheila Halasz, Ellen Javernick, Debbie Trafton O'Neal, Vicki Shannon, Terry Vermillion, and Christine Yount

Credits:
Edited by Susan L. Lingo
Cover designed by Liz Howe
Interior designed by Jill Christopher
Illustrations by Jan Knudson
Copyedited by Stephanie G'Schwind
Typeset by Kari Monson

Library of Congress Cataloging-in-Publication Data
Fun-to-learn Bible lessons. K-3 / [contributors, Nanette Goings... et al.].
         p.   cm.
      ISBN 1-55945-196-3 (v. 1)
      1. Bible—Study and teaching. 2. Christian education of children.
   I. Goings, Nanette.
   BS600.2.F86   1994
   268'.432—dc20   94-34358
                                                                    CIP

11 10 9 8 7 6 5 4 3 2   04 03 02 01 00 99 98 97 96 95

Printed in the United States of America.

Contents

Introduction

Welcome to a resource filled with exciting, active Bible lessons for kids in kindergarten through the third grade. Here are fun together-times that will grab your kids' attention and teach powerful lessons in building friendships, forging faith, nurturing forgiveness, and seeking God every day.

In *Fun-to-Learn Bible Lessons: K–3, Volume 1,* Sunday school teachers, vacation Bible school teachers, child-care directors, and anyone who has a heart for working with children will discover 20 simple-to-follow lessons which combine lively learning, active participation, songs, snacks, and colorful creations to make and take home.

As they focus on a selection of 20 Old and New Testament characters and the lessons they learned, children will experience exciting ways to apply each Bible story to their lives. You'll wind your way through Old and New Testament stories of

- courage and confidence,
- loyalty and love,
- promises and praises,
- fear and forgiveness,

and much more!

THE FUN-TO-LEARN LESSONS

Each lesson in *Fun-to-Learn Bible Lessons: K–3, Volume 1* contains five to seven exciting activities. Activities are fast-paced for children with short attention spans. The following elements are included in each lesson:

- **Introduction**—One or two paragraphs that provide an overview of the lesson's topic.
- **A Powerful Point**—A concise statement of the lesson's objective, telling what the children will learn.
- **A Look at the Lesson**—An outline including activity titles and estimated completion times. These times may vary according to your class size.
- **A Sprinkling of Supplies**—A list of all the items you'll need for the lesson.
- **The Fun-to-Learn Lesson**—Exciting, quick, Scripture-based activities. Kids experience each lesson through active learning using all five senses.

Lessons include interactive Bible stories, snappy action songs to familiar tunes, unique art projects, and simple snack ideas.

- **Handouts**—All necessary handouts are included. They're easy to use, and you have permission to photocopy them for local church use.

Get set to enjoy *Fun-to-Learn Bible Lessons: K–3, Volume 1*. Mix and match these Bible lessons for any gathering of children and watch your kids grow in confidence, friendships, and faith!

1. Losing Our Lonelies (Hagar)

Children can experience loneliness any time—even in a crowd. Friends are often too busy to play, parents are working, and brothers and sisters may be busy with other things. Children need to know that even when they're alone and feeling lost and friendless, God is with them. God is a companion who is never too busy or too far away.

Use this lesson to help your children understand God's promise to be with us wherever we go.

A POWERFUL POINT

We never need to feel lonely because God is with us.

A LOOK AT THE LESSON

1. "Left" Out (8 minutes)
2. Who's Missing? (7 minutes)
3. Hagar's Story (7 minutes)
4. A Walk in the Wilderness (8 minutes)
5. The Lonelies Left Me! (8 minutes)
6. Joy Cookies (9 minutes)

A SPRINKLING OF SUPPLIES

You'll need cellophane tape, a Bible, scissors, paper, crayons, a backpack, photocopies of the "You're Never Lost With God" handout (p. 11), and a chalkboard eraser. You'll also need unfrosted sugar cookies; frosting; plastic knives; and decorations such as raisins, peanuts, cereal bits, or colorful sprinkles.

THE FUN-TO-LEARN LESSON

1. "Left" Out

Before class, cut out two paper arrows for each child. As kids arrive, give them each two paper arrows. Have kids stand in a circle and put their arrows on the floor in front of them, each with one arrow pointing left and the other arrow pointing right. Tape the arrows in place.

Ask:

● **Who can tell about a time when you felt left out, maybe from a special party or a group of friends?**

● **How did you feel inside when that happened?**

Say: **Let's play a game to help us understand a little about what being left out might feel like. This game is like Musical Chairs, except you'll hop from arrow to arrow around the circle. You must hop on both feet and touch each arrow as you go around the circle. When the music stops, look at the arrow you're standing on. If it's pointing left, you're left out and must sit down in the center of the circle while we finish the game.**

Play until only one child is left or all the children have been "left out." Then gather children together and ask:

● **How did it feel to be left out?**

● **What can you do when you're feeling lonely or left out?**

Ask a volunteer to read Joshua 1:9 aloud. Ask:

● **What has God promised us in this verse?**

● **How does that promise make you feel?**

Say: **God has promised always to be with us wherever we go. That means we never need to feel lonely or left out or lost. God is a friend who's always with us.**

Have kids help you pick up the arrows and set them aside.

2. Who's Missing?

Say: **Sometimes we feel lonely when we miss someone who's special to us. Let's play a game about missing people and feeling lonely.**

Ask everyone to close and cover their eyes.

Say: **I'm going to tap some children on the shoulder. If I tap you, get up very quietly and go stand outside the room. Nobody peek!**

Choose two or three children to leave the room. Then have the other children open their eyes and take turns guessing who's missing. When the children guess the name of a missing person, have that child return. When the last child returns, ask him or her:

● **Were you the only person outside the room?** Accept either yes or no as an answer, then say: **I think someone was with** (name of child) **outside the room. Here's a riddle to help you know who it was. He is your friend. He loves you and has promised never to leave you alone.** Ask:

● **Do you know who it was?** (God.)

Say: **No one in this room or outside of this room is ever alone because God is always with you. No matter how lonely you may feel, God**

is always there.

3. Hagar's Story

(You'll need cellophane tape and photocopies of the "You're Never Lost With God" handout on page 11. Before you tell this story, cut one of the handouts apart. Hide the heart-shaped piece. Place the tape and the other puzzle pieces in a pile in front of a wall.)

Ask:

● **Who can tell about a time you were lost and couldn't find your parents?**

Say: **Being lost is really scary. Let's hear a Bible story about a woman and her little boy who were lost. As I tell you the story, you'll have a chance to help put our story puzzle together.**

Open your Bible to Genesis 21:14-19 and explain that this is where the story comes from.

Say: **Hagar was a servant girl in the house of Abraham and Sarah. Hagar had a little boy named Ishmael. One day Ishmael teased Sarah's son. Sarah was really angry and wanted Hagar and Ishmael to go away. So Abraham gave Hagar and Ishmael some food and water and sent them away into the desert.** Invite a child to choose any puzzle piece and tape it to the wall.

Hagar and Ishmael wandered in the desert and soon were lost. Hagar was lonely and afraid. Invite another child to add a second puzzle piece. **When the water was gone, Ishmael sat down under a bush and cried.** Have a child add a third puzzle piece. **Hagar cried, too. She cried because she was lonely. She cried because she was afraid. She cried because she was lost!** Have a child add a fourth puzzle piece. **But God heard their cries and**

sent an angel to help. **Hagar and Ishmael weren't really alone at all. God was with them.** Have a child add a fifth puzzle piece. Ask:

● **Why did Hagar and Ishmael feel lost?**

● **What has God promised us?**

Say: **It's time to put the missing piece in our puzzle.** Add the heart-shaped piece and ask a volunteer to read what's written on the puzzle.

Say: **Even when we're in strange, faraway places, God is with us. He never leaves us, so we don't have to feel lonely or afraid or lost.** Distribute photocopies of the "You're Never Lost With God" handout. **Here's a puzzle page for you to take home and cut apart. Invite your family to put the puzzle together as you tell them the story of Hagar and Ishmael. Save the heart-shaped piece for last, and as you put it in, tell your family that God is always with them.**

4. A Walk in the Wilderness

(You'll need slips of paper, crayons, and a backpack.)

Have children sit in a circle on the floor. Place the backpack in the center of the circle. Hand each child a crayon and a slip of paper. Ask:

● **Who can tell about a time you went hiking?**

● **What were some of the things you took along so you wouldn't get lost?**

Say: **We're going on a pretend hike in the wilderness. On your paper, draw a picture of something that keeps you from getting lost. When you're finished, place your picture in the backpack.** As the kids work on their pictures, draw a cloud with the word "God" on it. Place your picture in the backpack along with the children's

pictures.

When all the pictures are in the backpack, pass it around and let each child remove a paper and tell about what's on it and how it prevents them from getting lost.

When the backpack is empty, ask:

● **Which of these things can help us every time we're lost or lonely or afraid?** (God.)

● **Why is God the one we want to take along wherever we go?** (He promises us to always be there; he will help us if we are lonely or lost.)

5. The Lonelies Left Me!

(You'll need a chalkboard eraser.)

Gather children in a group on the floor. Place a chair in front of the children but not facing them.

Say: **Let's play a game to snatch away the lonelies. This eraser will be the lonelies. I'll pick one of you to sit in the chair with your back to the rest of the group. I'll put the lonelies under you. Then I'll tap someone to quietly tiptoe up and snatch away the lonelies. You'll have two guesses to find out who snatched them. If you guess right, you may change places with the snatcher.**

Be sure to play until everyone has been either a snatcher or a guesser. After the game, ask:

● **Who can snatch away our lonely feelings in real life?**

Say: **God will take away the lonelies and put smiles in our hearts instead.**

6. Joy Cookies

(Set out unfrosted sugar cookies; frosting; plastic knives; and decorating tidbits such as raisins, peanuts, and sprinkles.)

Ask:

● **Can we see God with our eyes?**

● **How do we know God is with us?**

Say: **We may not see God with our eyes, but we know he's always with us. God's love puts joy in our hearts and smiles on our faces. Let's celebrate our joy with "joy cookies" and show God how happy we are that he is always with us and we never have to feel alone.**

Allow children to decorate cookies with the goodies of their choice. When they're finished, have children carefully hold up their creations. Say: **Your joy cookies are beautiful! Each one is different and special, just like you are. God is always with us and thinks we're all very special. Let's thank God.**

Dear God, thank you for being with us when we feel lonely or lost or afraid. Thank you for promising to be with us wherever we go. In Jesus' name, amen.

by Sheila Halasz

YOU'RE NEVER LOST WITH GOD

2. No Time for Tricks (Jacob and Esau)

We all love to laugh, but kids need to learn that jokes and tricks aren't funny if they're at someone else's expense. A good laugh is only good when it's shared by everyone.

Jacob and Esau were biblical brothers who learned powerful lessons about the cost of a trick. Use this lesson to show children that God wants us to treat others with kindness, not trickery.

A POWERFUL POINT

God wants us to be kind and not play hurtful tricks.

A LOOK AT THE LESSON

1. Impossibly Tricky (8 minutes)
2. Tricky Touch (8 minutes)
3. Jacob and Esau Story (9 minutes)
4. Kind to You (9 minutes)
5. A Golden Reminder (9 minutes)
6. Love Is No Trick (7 minutes)

A SPRINKLING OF SUPPLIES

You'll need a Bible, reward stickers or small candies, fruit-flavored cereal, napkins, and a sack containing the following items: a piece of fake fur, a prune, a smooth stone, and cooked spaghetti in a small bowl. You'll also need two small sacks, pencils, slips of paper, two rulers, cellophane tape, two photocopies of the "Golden Rule" handout (p. 16), and photocopies of the "Love Is No Trick" handout (p. 16).

THE FUN-TO-LEARN LESSON

1. Impossibly Tricky

(You'll need reward stickers or small candies.)

Say: **I have a trick for you to try, and it sounds very simple. Raise your hand if you think you can lift your left foot.** Encourage each child to participate. (If you have a physically challenged child in your room, ask him or her to help you see if anyone can do this trick.)

Have kids spread out and find a place beside a wall in the classroom. Then say: **Stand sideways with your right shoulder and right foot touching the wall. Be sure to stand tall and straight. Now lean the right side of your head against the wall.** When children are in place, ask them to lift their left feet off the floor. No one will be able to do it! After everyone has tried, ask:

● **What's it like to not be able to do this simple trick?**

Say: **This trick couldn't be done, though it was kind of fun to try. But some tricks are mean.**

Ask:

● **Has anyone ever played a mean trick on you? What happened?**

● **How did it make you feel?**

Say: **God wants us to treat other people with love and kindness. We**

**want to do good things for people—
not make them feel bad with mean
tricks. I have something for each of
you because you've just learned a
tricky lesson!** Hand out the stickers
or candies.

2. Tricky Touch

(You'll need a large sack containing
a piece of fake fur, a smooth stone, a
prune, and cooked spaghetti in a bowl.)

Don't let kids see what's in the sack.
Seat children around you on the floor
and say: **Sometimes things are tricky
because they're not what you think
they are. Snakes are tricky because
you think they're slimy, but they're
really smooth and dry. Snakes are an
example of a tricky touch.**

Ask:

● **Who can think of another tricky
touch?** Allow kids to share responses,
which may include smooth wood that's
really splintery and soft mashed pota-
toes that are lumpy.

Then say: **Let's see if you're tricked
by the feel of things in this sack.
Reach in and feel each item but don't
tell out loud what you think it is. Be
careful not to peek. We'll let our fingers do the seeing until everyone's
had a turn.**

Allow kids to take turns reaching into the sack. When everyone's had a
chance to touch and guess, pull each
item from the sack to see if kids guessed
correctly.

Say: **Sometimes our sense of touch
can trick us. Let's hear a Bible story
about two brothers and a very tricky
touch.**

3. Jacob and Esau Story

(You'll need the smooth stone, the
piece of fake fur, the prune, and the
cooked spaghetti in a bowl.)

Seat kids at one end of the room.
Place the stone, the fur, the prune, and
the bowl of spaghetti on the floor at
the opposite end of the room facing
the kids. Ask:

● **Have you ever heard someone
say, "That was a dirty trick"?**

● **What do you think a dirty trick is?**

Open your Bible to Genesis 27. Hold
it up and say: **This story from the
Bible is about a tricky touch—and a
dirty trick. You can help me tell the
story of Jacob and Esau.**

**Whenever I say a word describing
a tricky touch, I'll signal to someone
to run to the other end of the room
and pick up the item that feels like
the word. For example, if I say
"hairy," you'll rush to grab the fur
piece and hold it up. Then set the
item down and return to your
place.** Go over each tricky-touch word
and item as follows.

Say: **If I say "hairy," you'll pick up
the fur piece.**

**If I say "smooth," you'll pick up
the smooth stone.**

**If I say "wrinkled," you'll pick up
the prune.**

**If I say "slippery," you'll pick up
the bowl of spaghetti.**

Say: **Let's begin our story. Long ago
in Bible times, Isaac and Rebekah
had two sons, named Esau and Jacob.
Esau was the oldest, and his skin was
very hairy.** (Pause.) **Jacob was his
twin, but he had smooth** (pause) **skin.
When Jacob and Esau's father was
old and wrinkled,** (pause) **he wanted
to give his hairy** (pause) **son, Esau, a
special blessing. This blessing was
only for the oldest boy in the family.
Since Jacob was not the oldest, this
made him angry and jealous. So
Jacob decided to play a slippery**
(pause) **trick and steal the blessing
meant for Esau.**

Jacob knew his father couldn't see very well, so he glued goat fur to his smooth (pause) **hands and neck. Then Jacob looked and felt like hairy Esau.** (Pause.) **Jacob dished up a bowl of slippery stew** (pause) **to take to his father for dinner. His father's wrinkled** (pause) **hand touched Jacob's hairy** (pause) **hand. Jacob's father thought it was Esau and gave his blessing. Jacob had tricked his father and brother. Jacob had stolen his brother's blessing with a slippery** (pause) **trick!**

Ask:

● **What did Jacob do to trick his brother and father?**

● **How do you think Esau felt when he learned how Jacob had stolen his blessing?**

● **Do you think it was a good idea to play this kind of trick? Why or why not?**

Say: **Jacob played a mean trick on Esau and his father. God wasn't happy with what Jacob did. God never tricks us, and God doesn't want us to trick others. God wants us to do kind things for others and not hurt them or do mean tricks.**

4. Kind to You

(You'll need two small sacks, pencils, and slips of paper.)

Gather kids in a circle on the floor. Hand each child a pencil and two slips of paper. On one slip, have them write their names. On the other slip, tell them to write or draw a picture of something kind they could do for someone. When everyone's finished, give two children each a sack. Ask one child to collect the slips of paper with the names. Have the other child collect the slips with the pictures. Say: **God wants us to be kind to other people and not trick them**

or be mean. I'll call on someone to come up and choose a name and a picture out of the sacks. You'll act out the kind action on the picture and the person whose name you drew will try to guess what that action is. Then that person may choose the next two slips of paper from the sacks.**

Continue until everyone's had a turn to choose a name and act out a picture. Say: **Isn't it wonderful that God's given us so many different ways to show kindness to others? Let's look at a very important verse in the Bible that tells us more about that.**

5. A Golden Reminder

(You'll need a Bible, fruit-flavored cereal, napkins, cellophane tape, two rulers, and two photocopies of the "Golden Rule" handout on page 16. Before starting this activity, color the rulers on the handouts yellow or gold then cut them out. Cut each ruler into 12 pieces using the inch marks as guidelines.)

Say: **God teaches us to treat other people the way we want to be treated. If we're kind to others, they'll be kind to us.**

Have a volunteer read aloud Matthew 7:12. Say: **This verse is called the golden rule. When we treat others as we want them to treat us, we'll shine with God's love!**

Form two teams and line up at one end of the room. Place a roll of tape and the two sets of ruler pieces you cut earlier at the opposite end of the room on a chair by the wall. Hold up the two real rulers. Say: **Let's have a relay race with these rulers. It'll help us practice being kind to others just as we want others to be kind to us. When I say "go," the first person on each** team will place a ruler on his or her head. Walk to the other end of the room and find the first inch of the Golden Rule on the chair. After you've taped the puzzle piece to the wall, return to your line so the next person can go. If the ruler drops off of your head, the person on the other team must help you replace it before going on. And you must help the other player if his or her ruler falls, too.

Play until both teams have taped their completed puzzles on the wall. Then say: **God wants us to treat each other kindly. When we're kind to others, they'll be kind to us. Let's practice serving one another kindly.**

Form small groups of three. Have a child from each group come up to get a napkin of cereal to serve someone in his or her group. The child who's been served will serve the next person in the group and so on. Have kids continue serving each other until everyone has a napkin with cereal. Remind the kids that being kind also means being polite. Have them say, "Thank you" as they're served.

Before eating the cereal, pray: **Dear God, we're sorry for the times we've hurt someone's feelings with tricks that were unkind. Help us remember that it's better to do kind things for people. And help us also remember to treat others the way we want to be treated. In Jesus' name, amen.**

6. Love Is No Trick

(You'll need a photocopy of the "Love Is No Trick" handout on page 16 for each child. Before this activity, cut off the portion of each handout with the hearts on it. The children will be using only the heart portion for this activity.)

With kids still seated in their small groups, ask:

● **If you wanted to show someone that you have the love of God in your heart, what could you do?**

Say: **When we do good things for other people, our hearts grow closer to God's heart. Let's end our time with a very nice kind of trick. I want to show you a way to make two hearts become one.**

Give each child a "Love Is No Trick" handout. Say: **Hold your paper away from you at arms' length. Look between the hearts and slowly begin to move your paper toward your nose.** The hearts will converge into one heart. Ask:

● **What do you see?**
● **What can we do to be closer to God?**
● **Why do you think God wants us to move closer to him?**

Say: **When we love others and do kind things for them, we show them God's love. God wants us to know that real love and treating others kindly is no trick! Join hands with the people in your group and let's say the golden rule together two times. "Do to others what you want them to do to you."** Repeat the verse once more.

by Sheila Halasz

THE GOLDEN RULE

Directions: Color the Golden Ruler yellow and cut it apart on the dotted lines. You'll need two sets of ruler pieces for kids to put together in a puzzle relay.

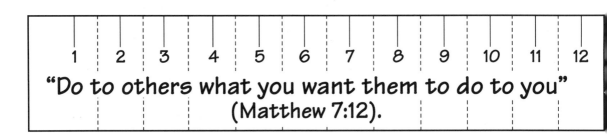

LOVE IS NO TRICK

1. Read the word on each heart.
2. Hold your paper at arms' length away.
3. Stare between the hearts and begin slowly moving the paper toward your nose.
4. What happens to the two hearts?

When we do good things for others, we move closer to God.

3. Getting Along With Brothers and Sisters (Joseph)

The Bible is filled with stories about problems between siblings—Cain and Abel, Jacob and Esau, Joseph and his brothers, and Rachel and Leah, just to name a few. Jealousy and envy were often at the heart of their problems. Many times, we too become angry with others—even our family members, like Joseph's brothers in the story of Joseph. Use this lesson to help kids learn that God wants us to treat our brothers and sisters with kindness.

A POWERFUL POINT

Family members need to be kind and forgiving.

A LOOK AT THE LESSON

1. Balloon Race (8 minutes)
2. A Bit of Background (6 minutes)
3. Hop, Step, and a Jump! (8 minutes)
4. Homemade Snacks (5 minutes)
5. Stand Up for Your Sisters and Brothers (5 minutes)
6. Give 'Em a Hand! (8 minutes)
7. I Ain't Gonna Fight No More (5 minutes)

A SPRINKLING OF SUPPLIES

Gather a bag of round balloons, a kitchen timer, a loaf of bread, peanut butter, plastic knives, napkins, and a Bible. You'll also need crayons or markers, and photocopies of the "Give 'Em a Hand!" handout (p. 21).

THE FUN-TO-LEARN LESSON

1. Balloon Race

(You'll need the balloons and the kitchen timer.)

Help children form pairs. Give each pair a balloon. Tell children that they'll need to work with their partners to carry their balloons to the other end of the room without using their hands. Demonstrate how they can squeeze a balloon between them, head to head or shoulder to shoulder. Have children line up at one end of the room with their partners. Set the timer for two minutes and explain that the race must be completed before the timer rings. If a balloon falls, the partners must pick it up and begin again at the starting line.

After the race, ask:

● **What did you and your partner have to do to finish the race?**

● **How did you feel if you or your partner dropped the balloon?**

● **Was it easy to forgive your partner when you knew you had to start over? Explain.**

Say: **At home, your brothers and sisters or other family members sometimes do things that bother you. God wants you to forgive them, too. Who can look up and read Matthew 18:21-22?** Pause as a child reads the verse.

Say: **Jesus said to forgive 77 times. That's a lot of forgiving!**

2. A Bit of Background

(You'll need a Bible.)

Open your Bible to Genesis 37 and 42–45 and show it to the children. Explain that you'll need everyone's help to tell the story.

Say: **God understands that we may get angry with our brothers and sisters sometimes. The Bible tells a story about a boy named Joseph who made his 11 brothers very angry.** (Have children say "Grrr!")

Joseph told his brothers, "In one of my dreams, you bowed down before me." (Have children make a low bow.)

Joseph's brothers were furious. (Have children repeat the growling noise.) **Joseph's brothers didn't want to bow down to Joseph—even in dreams. They were jealous of Joseph because of the beautiful coat their father had made for him. "Let's get rid of Joseph," said his brothers. So they threw poor Joseph into a well.** (Have children tumble to the floor.)

Soon, a group of men came by on their way to Egypt. Joseph's brothers decided to sell Joseph as a slave. The travelers took Joseph away to Egypt. (Have children walk slowly and sadly in place.)

Many years later, Joseph's brothers came to Egypt to beg for food. Show me how hungry they were. (Pause while children rub their tum-

mies.) **When they saw Joseph, they didn't recognize him.** (Have children act surprised.) **Joseph could have put his brothers in prison, but he didn't. Instead he said, "I am the brother you sold."**

Joseph's brothers were ashamed. "We didn't really mean to be so cruel to you, Joseph. We're sorry." said the brothers.

Joseph knew they were telling the truth. "I'll forgive you," he said. And to show how he forgave them, Joseph gave his brothers lots of food to take home for their hungry families.

After the story, ask:

● **Why do you think Joseph forgave his brothers?**

● **Do you think it was easy for Joseph to forgive them? Explain.**

● **How do you think God feels when we forgive our brothers and sisters?**

Say: **God understands we may get angry, but he wants us to work things out in a peaceful way.**

3. Hop, Step, and a Jump!

(You'll need a Bible.)

Have someone look up and read aloud 1 John 4:21. Then ask:

● **What are some ways to show love to your brothers, sisters, or other family members?**

● **What does the Bible teach us about how to treat the people in our families?**

Say: **God tells us that if we love him, we also need to love our brothers and sisters and treat them kindly. In this game, you'll have a chance to show that you know how to treat your brothers and sisters.**

Stand at one end of the room and have the children line up on the other side of the room.

Hold the Bible and say: **The Bible is God's Word and teaches us how to treat our brothers and sisters with kindness and love. When we're loving to our families, we grow closer to God. I'll suggest ways you might show kindness to your brothers and sisters. If what I say is kind and loving, hop three steps forward. If it's not loving, take a giant step backward. If I say something that you've done for someone in your family, jump up and down.**

Use these ideas:

● You washed your sister's muddy bike.

● Your brother accidentally broke your new watch, so you decide to break his model car.

● You prayed for your sister to get over the chicken pox.

● You made fun of your brother for getting a bad grade.

● You left the living room in a mess when company was about to come.

● You brought your mother breakfast in bed.

● You fought with your brother about which TV show to watch.

● You helped your dad make dinner on a night when he was really tired.

End by saying: **God wants us to treat our brothers and sisters with love and forgiveness. When we treat our families with love, we're helping to make a happy home.**

4. Homemade Snacks

(You'll need a loaf of bread, peanut butter, napkins, and plastic knives.)

Say: **Let's make some fun snacks to help us remember that God wants us to be kind to the people in our families.**

Allow children to spread peanut butter on one slice of bread and fold it over.

Have them cut their sandwiches into two squares. Then cut one square to make two triangles. Show them how to put the triangles together on top of the square to form a house with a roof.

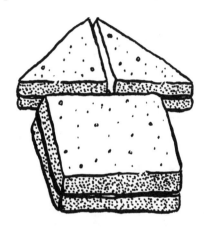

Say: **Listen to what Psalm 133:1 says: "It is good and pleasant when God's people live together in peace." As you eat your house snack, tell a partner something you can do this week to make your home a happy place.**

5. Stand Up for Your Sisters and Brothers

As children finish their snacks, help them form pairs and ask them to sit on the floor with their legs crossed. Ask:

● **Who can tell about a time when you were helped by a brother or sister?**

Say: **Now let's see if you can stand up without using your hands or asking anyone to help.**

Some kids may be able to do this, but most will find it difficult.

Say: **Some things are hard to do on our own, but when we have help, it's fun. Let's try some fun things with partners right now.**

Have partners try these stunts. It's best

for kids to choose partners of similar size.

● **Partner Pull-Ups**—Partners sit facing each other with feet touching, then reach forward and grasp hands. By pulling together, both come up to a standing position.

● **Partner Back-Ups**—Partners sit back to back, with arms hooked behind them and knees bent, then try to stand up by pushing against each other's back.

Say: **When we help each other, our work is much easier and more fun! God is always there helping us and we can be there to help others, too. Remember to give your sisters, brothers, and others a helping hand.**

6. Give 'Em a Hand!

(You'll need photocopies of the "Give 'Em a Hand!" handout on page 21 and crayons or markers.)

Ask:

● **What does it mean to give someone a "helping hand"?**

● **How do you think others feel when you help them?**

● **How does it make you feel to help someone in your family?**

Distribute the handouts and crayons or markers. Ask a volunteer to read the poem in the center of the page. Have kids cover the poem with one hand and trace around that hand.

Say: **Each time you give someone in your family a helping hand this week, write on one of the fingers the name of who you helped and what you did. Bring your paper back next week to share the ways you gave a helping hand.**

Remind kids to put their names on their handouts.

7. I Ain't Gonna Fight No More

As children finish working on their handouts, begin teaching these words to the tune of "It Ain't Gonna Rain No More." Have the children sing the first, second, and last lines with you. Have them listen as you sing the third line, then echo it back to you. (For extra fun, try acting out each verse as you sing it.)

"I AIN'T GONNA FIGHT NO MORE"

I ain't gonna fight no more, no more.
I ain't gonna fight no more.
When I play, I will share my toys.
(Echo)
I ain't gonna fight no more.

I ain't gonna tease no more, no more.
I ain't gonna tease no more.
When I talk, I'll say nice things.
(Echo)
I ain't gonna tease no more.

I ain't gonna grab no more, no more.
I ain't gonna grab no more.
I won't take things 'til I say "please."
(Echo)
I ain't gonna grab no more.

I ain't gonna push no more, no more.
I ain't gonna push no more.
I'll wait in line and take my turn.
(Echo)
I ain't gonna push no more.

I'll act just like our Lord, our Lord.
I'll act just like our Lord.
And love my brothers and sisters, too.
(Echo)
I'll act just like our Lord.

Close with a prayer and remind the children to bring back their "Give 'Em a Hand" handouts next week.

by Ellen Javernick

GIVE 'EM A HAND

1. Lay your hand over the poem in the center of the page, then trace around your hand.

2. Each time you help someone in your family, write that person's name
and how you helped on one of your traced fingers.

3. Bring your paper next week to share the ways you
gave your family members a helping hand.

I really love my family, and
I'll give them all a helping hand!

4. 'Specially ME! (Moses)

Moses accomplished extraordinary feats with God's power. Through God, Moses turned a wooden staff into a snake, commanded water to turn into blood, and even parted the Red Sea for the Israelites to cross. But Moses suffered from self-doubt. Moses thought he wasn't special enough to be used by God. You might say Moses had a bad case of the "I can'ts."

As you share the story of Moses and how God used Moses' unique talents, children will learn that God created them to be special, too. Use this lesson to help children leave behind "I can'ts" and go on to real "CANfidence" in God.

A POWERFUL POINT

God made each of us special.

A LOOK AT THE LESSON

1. Snatch the Can (7 minutes)
2. Moses Is Special (9 minutes)
3. Food From Heaven (9 minutes)
4. Picture-Perfect Gifts (9 minutes)
5. Spin a Special Word (9 minutes)

A SPRINKLING OF SUPPLIES

Gather an empty can, seven 3×5 cards, a Bible, graham crackers, honey, two plastic knives, napkins, cellophane tape, scissors, markers, an empty soft drink bottle, small bows, and one photocopy of the "Picture-Perfect Present" handout (p. 26) for each child.

THE FUN-TO-LEARN LESSON

1. Snatch the Can

(You'll need an empty can.)

Form two teams with the children. Say: **God's given us so many special talents and gifts. We know that with God helping us, we can always say, "I can."** Hold up the empty can. **Let's play a game with this can to show that we really "can"!**

Set a chair in the front of the room. Place the empty can on the chair. Have teams sit on the floor in front of the chair. Choose a child from each team to stand on either side of the chair so the can is in the middle. Say: **I'm going to call out an action to do. The first person to snatch the can and shout, "I can!" will have a chance to do that action. Everyone on that person's team must cheer while he or she tries. Then the other person will have a chance to see if he or she can do that action, too.**

Call out the following actions or create some of your own:

● **Hop on one foot to another child and shake his or her hand.**

● **Say the alphabet backward.**

● **Close your eyes and touch your finger to your nose.**

● **Wiggle your nose and ears at the same time.**

● **Skip backward around the classroom.**

● **Write your name with your other hand.**

● **Tie someone's shoes with your eyes closed.**

Continue until everyone's had a chance to play Snatch the Can. Then seat the children in a circle on the floor and ask:

● **Why do you think God gives us each different talents?**

● **How can we use our talents to help others?**

Say: **Each of us has different gifts from the Lord. They're part of what makes you special. Today we'll hear a story about a man who wasn't sure he was special.**

2. Moses Is Special

(You'll need a Bible and cellophane tape. Before this activity, write one letter of the word "special" on each of seven 3×5 cards. Scatter the cards face up and randomly on the floor. Set a roll of tape nearby.)

Gather the children around the cards. Say: **Sometimes it's hard for us to believe that we're special and that we can do special things.**

Ask:

● **Who can tell about a time when you were afraid to try something new?**

Say: **Sometimes we're afraid to try new things because we think we'll look silly. Sometimes we say, "I can't" before we even try!**

Open your Bible to Exodus 4:10-16. Hold it up and say: **Even people in the Bible had the "I can'ts" sometimes. Today we'll hear a story about Moses and how God helped Moses see how special he was. As I tell the story, I'll say some words very loudly. If you know what letter that word begins with, put your hand on your head. I'll call on someone to find the letter and tape it to the wall.** By the story's

end, the letters on the wall will spell out the word "special."

Say: **Moses was chosen by God to lead God's people out of *SLAVERY*** (call on a child to put up the letter S) **in Egypt. God wanted Moses to talk to the Egyptian king, who was called Pharaoh. God wanted Moses to tell Pharaoh to free God's *PEOPLE*.** (Choose a child to put up the letter P.) **But Moses was afraid. He didn't think he could speak well. Moses didn't think he was special *ENOUGH*.** (Choose a child to put up the letter E.) **Moses said to God, "I *CAN'T*."** (Call on a child to put up the letter C.) **God said to Moses, "Who made you? Who created your mouth to speak? Who made you special? *I*** (have a child put up the letter I) **did." Moses knew God was right. God had made Moses, and God would help him. God sent Moses' brother *AARON*** (call on a child to put up the letter A) **to help Moses speak to Pharaoh. Moses knew then how special he was because God *LOVED*** (call on a child to put up the letter L) **him and helped him do hard things.**

Ask:

● **Who can read what our word says? It tells what Moses was, and it tells what you are, too.**

● **Why did Moses have the "I can'ts" at the beginning of the story?**

● **Why did Moses feel special by the end of the story?**

● **Why was Moses able to do God's work even though he first said, "I can't"?**

Say: **We know that God made us and that God is always ready to help us. That means we never have to say, "I can't." Because God made us special, we can always say, "I can!"**

3. Food From Heaven

(You'll need graham crackers, honey, napkins, and two plastic knives.)

Ask:

● **Can anyone tell about a time when your mom or dad cooked your favorite meal or made a special treat just for you?**

● **How did you feel when you were treated so specially?**

Say: **God made all people special. After Moses helped free God's people from Pharaoh, they wandered in the wilderness with no food to eat, and they were hungry. Show me what it sounds like when a tummy growls for food!** (Pause for kids to "rrrumble.")

Continue, saying: **But God took care of his people because they were special. God sent food from heaven called manna. Manna was a sticky, white food that clung to the bushes and had to be picked off to eat. Manna probably tasted something like graham crackers and sweet honey. The word "manna" means "what is it?"** That's a good name because the people probably wondered what they were eating!

Ask:

● **Why do you think God wanted to give something as special as manna to Moses and the others?**

● **How could the people have thanked God for such a special food?**

Say: **Let's make a special treat that tastes a lot like manna must have tasted.** Set out graham crackers, honey, napkins, and plastic knives. Let the children take turns spreading honey on their crackers. Before children enjoy their treat, pray: **Dear Father, we thank you for making us special. You always help us and give good things to us because we're special in your eyes. In Jesus' name, amen.**

4. Picture-Perfect Gifts

(You'll need scissors, cellophane tape, markers, small bows, and photocopies of the "Picture-Perfect Present" handout on page 26. You may wish to photocopy the handouts onto heavier paper.)

Say: **God has given us many special gifts as part of the wonderful world we live in. I'll name a few of these gifts and then let's see if you can name some.** (Gifts might include Jesus, seashells, animals, clouds, and stars.) Encourage each child to name a gift God has given.

Say: **In our class today, there are** (number of people, including yourself) **very special gifts from God. Do you know who they are?** Pause for responses.

Have children form pairs. Hand each child a photocopy of the "Picture-Perfect Present" handout. Have someone read the verse on the box aloud. Ask:

● **How does this Bible verse help us know that we're special gifts from God?**

Say: **Because God loves us, he made each of us special. Let's make gift boxes to show that each of us is a gift from God.**

Direct the children to cut out the cross shape on the handout. Help kids find the box where they'll draw their faces with markers. (If you have access to an instant-print camera, you may wish to use photos of the children. Glue the photographs where the children would draw their faces.)

Place the paper cross so the printed side is up. Show the children how to fold downward on the dotted lines to make a box. Be sure children's drawings are on the inside bottom of the boxes. Have children work together to help each other tape the sides of their gift boxes. Make sure they don't tape the lids closed. Then invite them each to choose a bow to stick on the top of their boxes.

When everyone's finished, say: **God wants you to know how special you are to him. You can open your gift box any time and see a precious present God's given to us—you!**

5. Spin a Special Word

(You'll need one empty soft drink bottle.)

To end class time, ask children to sit down and join you in a circle on the floor. Place the bottle in the center of the circle.

Say: **It's always nice when someone tells us we're special and says something nice about our talents.**

Ask:

● **Why is it good to encourage others?**

Say: **Let's end our time with a fun game called Spin a Special Word. I'll spin this bottle, and we'll see who it points to.** Spin the bottle and wait to see who it points to. (Use the bottle neck as the pointer.) Then turn to that child and say: (Name), **you're special because . . .** Complete the sentence by saying something special about that child.

Say: **Each of you will have a turn to spin the bottle and say something encouraging to someone.**

Allow the child you just affirmed to spin the bottle next. Continue around the circle until everyone's been affirmed. Then ask:

● **How did you feel when someone said that you were special?**

● **How did you feel when you gave a special compliment?**

● **When is a good time to remind your friends and family that they're each a special gift from God?**

End with this prayer: **Dear God, thank you for the special friends who are here. Please help us remember that you love each and every one of us because we're your children. Help each of us to say, "I can do whatever God asks because God thinks I'm special." In Jesus' name we pray, amen.**

by Debbie Trafton O'Neal

PICTURE-PERFECT PRESENT

1. Cut out the cross shape.

2. Draw yourself on the **back** of the marked square.

3. With the printed side up, fold downward on the dotted lines.

4. Tape your gift box together at the sides. Don't tape the lid closed.

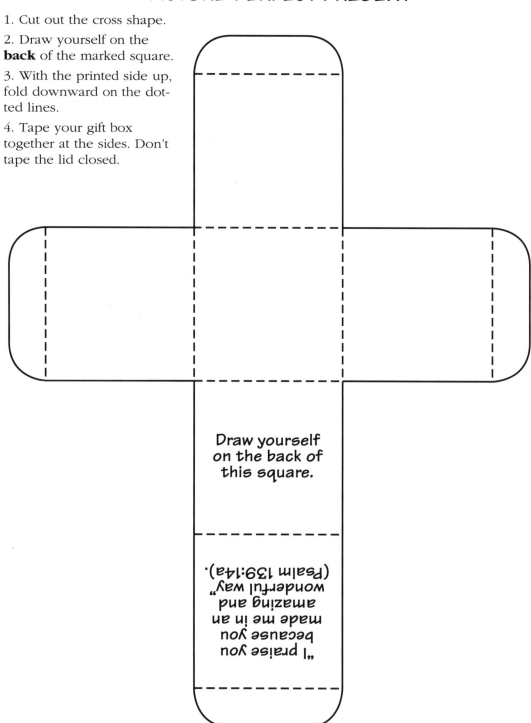

Draw yourself on the back of this square.

"I praise you because you made me in an amazing and wonderful way" (Psalm 139:14a).

5. God Is Always Near (Caleb)

The Bible says true faith is believing in what can't be seen. God's great soldiers, Caleb and Joshua, had faith that went far beyond what their eyes could see. They knew God was with them and would give them victory even when the other soldiers could see nothing but insurmountable obstacles.

It's hard for us to believe in what we can't see. Use this lesson to help build children's faith in knowing that God is here even if we can't see him with our eyes.

A POWERFUL POINT

God is with us no matter where we are.

A LOOK AT THE LESSON

1. Now You See It (6 minutes)
2. Fun Fans (7 minutes)
3. Spy Time (6 minutes)
4. Fruit of the Land (6 minutes)
5. "I Spy" Scripture (8 minutes)
6. Caleb Chorus (5 minutes)
7. Thanks for Being Here (4 minutes)

A SPRINKLING OF SUPPLIES

You'll need a balloon for each child, colored paper, crayons or markers, a Ping-Pong ball, a stapler, a Bible, and one medium-sized cluster of seedless grapes. You'll also need to gather a large sheet of white poster board, rulers (one for every pair of children), cellophane tape, a marker, and purple and green construction paper.

THE FUN-TO-LEARN LESSON

1. Now You See It

(You'll need one balloon for each child.)

Gather kids around you on the floor and ask this riddle:

● **What is all around us and over us and under us and inside of us—but can't be seen?** Pause for children to offer answers. (The answer to the riddle is "air.")

Ask:

● **If we can't see it, how do we know air is real?**

● **Can you think of any way to show air is real?**

Listen to responses and ideas, then hand each child a balloon. Blow up the balloons and tie the ends. You'll need to help younger children. Then ask:

● **How do we know there's air inside these balloons?**

● **Do the balloons look different with air inside? How?**

Say: **Let's play a game with our balloons.** Form two lines at one end of the room for a relay.

Say: **Tap your balloon up in the air as you walk to the other end of the room. If your balloon touches the floor, come back and start again. Bounce your balloon in the air back**

27

to your line. Then the next person in line will have a turn.

Continue playing until all the children have had a turn. Set the balloons aside and sit in a circle with the kids. Say: **Balloons help us know air is in the room. We know God is here, too. The way we act helps us know God is working in our lives. When we're kind to others, we know God's helping us. Let's find out more about trusting what we can't see.**

2. Fun Fans

(You'll need colored paper, a stapler, markers or crayons, and a Ping-Pong ball.)

Say: **We can't see the air, but we know it's here. Blow on your hand and feel the air move.** Try this with your kids, then ask:

● **What are some other ways to see how air moves?** Brainstorm ideas such as windmills, ceiling fans, and cars whizzing past.

Say: **We know air is real because of what it does and how it feels. Let's create our own way to make air move by making fun fans.**

Hand out sheets of colored paper and encourage children to decorate them with markers or crayons. Demonstrate how to fold the paper accordion-style to make a fan. Staple one end of the fan for a handle.

Sit with kids in a big circle on the floor. Say: **Let's try to blow a Ping-Pong ball around our circle. Fan the ball with your fan and roll the ball to the person sitting beside you.**

When the ball has traveled around the circle, ask:

● **How did the ball move so well?**

● **How is the way air moves like the way God can move in our lives?**

Say: **Sometimes it's hard to remember that God is here because we can't see God with our eyes. Now you'll hear a story about a very special man who was sure God was with him even though he couldn't see God with his eyes.**

3. Spy Time

(You'll need a Bible.)

Open your Bible to Numbers 13. Say: **This story is about men who were spies for God.**

Ask:

● **Can anyone explain what a spy is?**

● **Why do people spy?**

Say: **You can help me tell this story by learning some words to repeat. The words you'll say are "good, bad, strong, or weak." Let's say those words together. Ready?** Repeat these words a few times with your kids so they'll be familiar with them.

Say: **I'll tell you when to say the story words. Let's begin our story about Caleb, God's spy. God wanted to give his people a special, new land. But first, God told some spies to sneak into this new land to see if it was...** (say the story words). **He wanted the spies to see if the people who lived in this new land were...** (repeat the story words).

Caleb was one of God's spies, and he was a man who loved God very much. Caleb knew that God was with him all the time, no matter if he was... (say the story words). **When the spies reached the new land, they saw that it was rich and filled with good food. They picked some grapes to take home to show how good the land was. But Caleb and the other spies also saw that no matter whether the people were...** (say the story words), **they would fight to keep their**

land.

When the spies returned, God's people said, "**Tell us about the new land. Is it...** (repeat the story words).

When they heard that the people were strong and would fight, everyone except Caleb and Joshua grumbled and grouched to God. "**Why did you bring us here to fight when we will surely lose?**" they cried.

But Caleb knew God was always with them and would help them win the battle. And they did win! Caleb knew God was always with him whether Caleb was... (repeat the story words).

Say: **The same is true for us. No matter what, God is always here for us.**

4. Fruit of the Land

(You'll need the Bible and a medium-sized cluster of seedless grapes.)

Seat children with you in a circle on the floor. Say: **Caleb was a man of great faith.** Hold up your Bible and point to it. **Let's find out what the Bible says about faith.** Ask a volunteer to look up and read aloud Hebrews 11:1. Ask:

● **What is faith?**

● **Do we believe in only what we can see?**

● **What made Caleb a man of great faith?**

Say: **Caleb believed God was with him, even though he couldn't see God. Caleb saw the wonderful things God made, like beautiful stars, powerful rivers, and rich land with ripe grapes like these.** Hold up the grapes.

Say: **I'm going to pick a grape and tell one way I know God is here.** Pluck a grape. **I know God is here because I see God in each of you.**

Pass the grapes around the circle and allow children to say how they sense God's presence. Continue until all the grapes are gone and say: **Because we have faith, we know God is with us everywhere.**

5. "I Spy" Scripture

(You'll need cellophane tape, a ruler for every two kids, a large sheet of white poster board, a marker, and purple and green construction paper.)

Before this activity, you'll need to cut 10 grapes from purple construction paper and 10 grapes from green construction paper. Make each construction paper grape a 2-inch-wide oval.

Say: **Caleb and the other spies picked grape clusters to bring back to their people. The clusters were so big, they had to carry them between two poles! God let the spies find these juicy grapes so they would know how good the land was.**

Just as God gave grapes to the spies as proof of his blessings, God gives us Scripture as part of his blessings. Let's see if we can be Scripture spies.

Form pairs, hand each pair a ruler, and have them sit on the floor. Say: **Cover your eyes, and I'll hide 20 purple and green grapes around the room. Then you and your partner will go on a spy hunt! Each of you will hold an end of the ruler, just as Caleb did when he helped carry a pole for the heavy grapes. When you find a grape, place it on your ruler and walk back to your seat. If you drop the grape, set it back on the ruler and continue. If you have time, you can hunt for another grape. Ready? Now don't peek, or we won't have as much fun.**

After kids' eyes are hidden, quickly tape the grapes in plain sight around the room. If your group is older, make the hiding places a bit more obscure. When you're finished, tell kids to hold onto the ends of their rulers and begin the hunt.

When all the grapes have been found, tape them in a cluster on a large sheet of poster board. Invite each child to write his or her name on a grape. Title your poster "We Have a BUNCH of Faith in God!" (Your poster will make a wonderful display in your classroom or hallway.)

Say: **When we have faith, we know God's with us even when we can't see him.**

6. Caleb Chorus

Have children stand up and spread out around the room for this active singalong song.

Say: **I have a fun song to share with you about Caleb's mighty faith. I'll sing it to you once and show you the actions that go with it. Then we'll practice a few times.**

Sing "Caleb Chorus" to the tune of "Twinkle, Twinkle, Little Star."

"CALEB CHORUS"

Caleb's faith was mighty strong; *(flex muscles)*
tall and *(arms high in air)*
deep and *(one hand touching floor*

and other in air)
wide and *(arms out wide at sides)*
long!*(Lean forward with arms stretched out front.)*

He spied for God *(hands cupped over eyes)*
and searched the land; *(hands parting pretend bushes)*
he brought back grapes *(hand rubbing stomach in circular motion)*
in both his hands. *(Hold palms upward.)*

Caleb's faith was mighty strong; *(flex muscles)*
tall and *(arms high in the air)*
deep and *(one hand touching floor and other in the air)*
wide and *(arms out wide at sides)*
long! *(Lean forward with arms stretched out front.)*

Practice the song and actions with your kids so they're comfortable with them. Then substitute the children's names for Caleb's. Try speeding up the song with each name. For extra excitement and challenge, do the actions in place of singing the action words.

7. Thanks for Being Here

(You'll need a Bible.)
Have kids sit on the floor. Ask:
● **What are some of the ways we can see God without using our eyes?** Answers may include feeling him work and move in our lives, seeing the things God created, and reading Scripture.

Say: **There's another way we see God. It's through prayer. Sometimes when we pray, we can just be quiet and listen as God speaks to us.**

Have a volunteer read Psalm 100:3 aloud. Say: **Let's take a moment to be still and know that the Lord is God. Bow your head and close your eyes**

and be very still. Allow a few moments of silence, then close with a prayer similar to this one: **Dear God, help us to have the faith of Caleb. Help us know you're always with us even if we can't see you with our eyes. We love you, God. In Jesus' name, amen.**

Let children each take a balloon home with them to explain to their families that God is always with us, even if we can't see him, just like we know there's air in a balloon even though we can't see it.

by Vicki Shannon

6. Never Fear—God Is Here!
(Gideon)

In the book of Judges, Gideon faced fear and insecurity. He wanted God's reassurance over and over. With love and patience, God answered Gideon's questions, and Gideon learned to put his trust in God.

Loneliness, sorrow, anger, and insecurity are feelings related to fear. When kids are afraid or insecure, they look for things that are familiar to them. Use this lesson to reassure kids that God will help us whenever we're unsure or afraid.

A POWERFUL POINT

God will help us when we're fearful.

A LOOK AT THE LESSON

1. Faith Fall (5 minutes)
2. Gideon's Help (9 minutes)
3. T-R-U-S-T (7 minutes)
4. The Shadow Chaser (8 minutes)
5. Afraid Charades (9 minutes)
6. In God We Trust (8 minutes)

A SPRINKLING OF SUPPLIES

Collect a Bible, a roll of masking tape, five 3×5 cards, a black marker, a flashlight, and a small bag of candy hearts.

THE FUN-TO-LEARN LESSON

1. Faith Fall

(You'll need masking tape.)

Before you begin this activity, clear a space next to a wall. Place a 6-foot strip of masking tape on the floor parallel to the wall and about six feet in front of it.

For this activity, you'll need to pair children up according to size. Say: **Trust is being sure of something. But trusting isn't always easy. Decide with your partner which one of you will stand on the starting line. The other person will stand about a foot behind you. When I say "go," the person on the line will fall backward and the other partner will catch him or her. Be sure to keep your body stiff when you fall.**

Let kids switch roles. When both partners have fallen backward, group kids in a circle on the floor. Ask:

● **Who are people you trust?**
● **Why is it hard to trust when we're afraid?**

Say: **God wants us to put our trust in him. When we trust God, we don't need to be afraid of anything. Today we'll hear a Bible story about a soldier who was afraid to trust God.**

2. Gideon's Help

(You'll need a Bible.)
Sit in a circle on the floor and ask:

● **Who can share about a time you felt afraid?**
● **Why does it make us feel better to have someone near when we're afraid?**

Open your Bible to Judges 6:36-40.

Say: **In the Bible, you'll find lots of stories about people who were afraid. But God taught the people to trust him. You can help tell this story by learning some simple action words.**

Teach kids this simple pattern: slap (gently slap thighs), clap (softly clap hands), and stomp (stomp feet). As you tell the Bible story, they'll be repeating this pattern with the following words:

Do (slap thighs) **not** (clap hands) **fear** (stomp feet); **I** (slap thighs) **am** (clap hands) **here** (stomp the floor)!

Practice the action words several times together until children are comfortable with them. Then say: **I'm going to tell you a story about one of God's soldiers. The soldier was named Gideon. God wanted Gideon to be brave and battle for his people's freedom. But Gideon didn't feel brave. He was afraid. Show me a face that looks afraid.** (Pause for kids to respond.) **Gideon wanted to be sure God was with him. He asked God, "How will I know you'll be with me?" And God told Gideon, "Do** (slap) **not** (clap) **fear** (stomp); **I** (slap) **am** (clap) **here** (stomp)!"

But Gideon still wasn't sure. He spread the wool from a sheep on the ground and said, "God, if you're with me, make the ground wet but keep this wool dry." And God made the ground wet and kept the wool dry. It was God's way of saying to Gideon, "Do (slap) **not** (clap) **fear** (stomp); **I** (slap) **am** (clap) **here** (stomp)!"

Ask:

● **Do you think this was the last time Gideon questioned God? Let's find out!**

Say: **Because Gideon was so afraid of doing the wrong thing, he asked God one more time. Gideon said,** "God, if you're really with me, please make the ground dry and the wool wet." And God did this for Gideon. Again, it was God's way of saying, "Do (slap) not (clap) fear (stomp); I (slap) am (clap) here (stomp)!"

Finally Gideon trusted God and went into battle. God was with Gideon, and his people won the battle.

After kids have heard the story of Gideon, ask:

● **What did Gideon learn about God?**

Have a child read Judges 6:16 aloud. Say: **When we're afraid, we can be like Gideon and trust God. God is always with us. Let's say our special action words three more times to help us remember what God promises. "Do** (slap) **not** (clap) **fear** (stomp); **I** (slap) **am** (clap) **here** (stomp)!" (Repeat two more times.)

3. T-R-U-S-T

(You'll need five 3×5 cards and a black marker.)

Before this activity, write each the following letters on a separate 3×5 card: T, R, U, S, and T.

Ask the children if they're familiar with the song "Bingo." Choose five children to come and each hold a letter card. Be sure the card holders position themselves so that the children sitting down can read the word "trust." Say: **We'll sing this song to the tune of "Bingo." When we come to the letters, the card holders will hop forward each time their letters are sung. The second time we sing the song, the person holding the T card will hide it, and the rest of us will clap instead of singing the letter T. Each time we repeat the song, we'll hide another letter until every card is hidden and we're clapping the letters in-**

stead of singing them.

Lead the children in singing "Trust" to the tune of "Bingo."

"TRUST"

**When I have fears
or I'm afraid,
I'll put my trust in God. Oh—
T-R-U-S-T!
T-R-U-S-T!
T-R-U-S-T!
I'll put my trust in God! Oh!**

**When I have fears
or I'm afraid,
I'll put my trust in God. Oh—
(Clap) R-U-S-T!
(Clap) R-U-S-T!
(Clap) R-U-S-T!
I'll put my trust in God! Oh!**

Continue in the same way until you're clapping each letter.

4. The Shadow Chaser

(You'll need a flashlight, a Bible, and access to a room that can be darkened.)

Gather the children in a darkened corner of the room next to a wall and ask this riddle:

● **What's black but never white and disappears with morning light?** (The answer is "shadows.")

Give kids time to guess. If no one comes up with the answer, say: **I'll give you a clue to our riddle, but you'll have to use your eyes.** Ask a child to turn off the lights. Then turn on the flashlight and make a hand shadow on the wall by holding the light in front of your hand. Then ask the children what they see (a shadow). Ask:

● **Who can tell about a time when a shadow seemed scary? Tell us why you were afraid.**

Say: **Let's take turns making shadows on our wall!** Call on one child at a time to come up and make a hand shadow as you hold the flashlight. Encourage the others to guess what shape the shadow makes.

Say: **Sometimes shadows can seem frightening because they're big and dark and we don't know what object is making the shadow. But God is the shadow chaser! He's always with us, and God never changes.** Open the Bible to Joshua 1:9. Have a volunteer read the verse aloud. Say: **God promises to always be with us, and he'll help us not be scared of anything!**

5. Afraid Charades

Say: **Acting out the things that scare us can make us feel less afraid. I'm going to choose someone who'd like to come up and act out something that a lot of us are afraid of. I'll whisper it to that person, then he or she will act it out. The rest of you can try to guess what that fear is. Then someone else may have a turn.**

If some kids don't want to act, allow them to choose another child to take their place. Being in front of others can be a fear in itself! Whisper these fears to the children:

● **Going to bed at night.**
● **Climbing a tall ladder.**
● **Seeing a snake.**
● **Riding a roller coaster.**
● **Hearing thunderstorms.**
● **Swimming.**
● **Riding a bike.**
● **Taking a test.**
● **Riding in an airplane.**
● **Facing a bully.**

Say: **God is always with us. And when we trust God, we know he'll help us not be afraid.**

6. In God We Trust

(You'll need a bag of candy hearts.)

Form pairs. Give each child three candy hearts. Tell kids not to eat their candy hearts yet. Say: **Think of a fear you'd like to get rid of. If you wish, you may share that fear with your partner.** Pause for a few seconds to allow time for the children to share if they wish.

Then say: **I'm going to say a sentence for you to repeat. Then you and your partner may trade a candy heart and eat it. Ready? "I want to give my fears to God."** Pause while kids repeat the sentence and exchange hearts. **"I want to give my trust to God."** Let children repeat the sentence and exchange hearts. **"I want to give my love to God."** Pause for children to repeat the sentence and exchange hearts.

Say: **Find another pair of partners and join hands with them. Let's say a prayer thanking God for being with us and taking away our fears. Dear God, we thank you for being bigger than our fears. We're so glad you're always with us and that you'll help us when we're afraid. Help us have more trust in you, God. In Jesus' name, amen.**

by Debbie Trafton O'Neal

7. Friends Stick Together (Ruth and Naomi)

Few things in life are as precious as close friends. The Bible is filled with stories of great friends, such as David and Jonathan, Jesus and John, and Ruth and Naomi. The story of Ruth and Naomi emphasizes the loyalty of close friends and how God plays a major role in their lives together.

The way God loves us teaches us how to love our friends. Just as our faithfulness is a way to show love to God, loyalty is one way to show love to friends. Use this lesson to help children understand how being loyal helps build loving friendships.

A POWERFUL POINT

Good friends are loyal to each other.

A SPRINKLING OF SUPPLIES

You'll need a box of cereal, one large bowl, two paper cups, two paper plates, two plastic spoons, and a feather. You'll also need a Bible, a spool of thread, embroidery floss, scissors, seed beads, cupcake papers, newsprint, a marker, and several rolls of Life Savers candy.

A LOOK AT THE LESSON

1. Harvesting the Grain (9 minutes)
2. Friends Stick Together (7 minutes)
3. Ruth and Naomi (8 minutes)
4. Friendship Bracelets (8 minutes)
5. A Friendship Song (5 minutes)
6. Loyal to Others, Loyal to God (7 minutes)

THE FUN-TO-LEARN LESSON

1. Harvesting the Grain

(You'll need a box of cereal, two paper cups, two paper plates, two plastic spoons, and one large bowl.)

Have kids sit in a large circle. Place the bowl in the center of the circle and fill it with cereal. On either side of the bowl, place the paper plates with a cup on each. Hold the plastic spoons and say: **In Bible times, many people who were poor had to eat leftover grain that was dropped by the harvesters. This was called gleaning. Let's play the Gleaning Game. I'll hand two people each a spoon. They'll have 30 seconds to spoon cereal out of the bowl and into the cups. Whatever they harvest, they may eat!**

Hand the spoons to two kids and give them 30 seconds to harvest the cereal. When time is up, empty the cereal in the cups into the children's hands for them to munch on. Then say: **Before we pick two more kids to harvest grain, I want you to look at the cereal that's left on the plates. This is the gleaned grain. I'll divide this gleaned grain among the rest of you to eat later.**

Hand the spoons to two more children. Continue in this way until everyone's had a chance to harvest some grain. Then divide the grain remaining on the paper plates between the children. Let them enjoy the gleaned grain.

36

Say: **Later I'll share a Bible story about two very good friends. One of the friends gleaned the grain from fields to keep both of them from going hungry. These were two friends who really stuck together. Friends who stick together are loyal to each other. Let's see what that's like.**

2. Friends Stick Together.

(You'll need a feather.)

Hold up the feather and ask:

● **Who can tell us the meaning of the saying "Birds of a feather flock together"?**

Say: **When friends are loyal to each other, they stick together. If one friend feels sad, the other feels sad and tries to cheer his or her friend up. We're going to be birds of a feather today. I'll pair you with a partner, and we'll have fun sticking together.**

Form pairs and have them stand back to back at one end of the room. If there are three in a team, have them stand back to back in a triangle shape. Instruct kids to link their arms together at the elbows. Place the feather at the opposite end of the room from where kids are standing.

Say: **When I say "go," you and your partner will walk forward and try to be the first team to snatch this feather. You must stay stuck together. If you become separated, you must return to the starting place and begin again. Ready?**

Play this game through a few times. Then call kids back to the center of the room and ask:

● **What did it take to play this game?**

● **How did it feel to be stuck to your friend?**

Say: **Being loyal means we work**

together and stick together. It also means we think of the other person before we think of ourselves. God wants us to be loyal and kind to our friends. I'd like to share a Bible story with you about two friends from the same family. They stuck together and helped each other during hard times. They were loyal friends.

3. Ruth and Naomi

(You'll need a Bible and a spool of thread.)

Have kids sit with you in a circle while you tell this story. Hold on to your Bible and the spool of thread.

Ask:

● **Who'd like to share about a best friend?**

Hold up your Bible and point out the book of Ruth. Say: **In the Bible, there's a wonderful story about two people who were very good friends. Their names were Ruth and Naomi.** Now hold up the thread and say: **As I tell the Bible story, we'll pass this spool of thread around our circle. When I say "stop," the person holding the spool will tell in his or her own words the part of the story I just told. As you re-tell it, unwind the thread. When I begin the story again, we'll continue passing the spool. We'll let the end of the thread dangle along, so try to keep the thread from breaking.**

Pass the spool to the first child on your right and say: **Ruth was a young woman. She and her friend Orpah married two brothers. The mother of those two men was called Naomi. Stop.** (Have the child holding the spool of thread retell this portion of the story in his or her own words while unwinding the thread.)

Start the spool around the circle again and continue: **Ruth and her husband**

and Orpah and her husband and Naomi all lived together happily in the land of Moab. (Have the child holding the spool of thread retell this portion of the story while unwinding some more thread.)

Pass the spool and continue the story, saying: **Then an awful thing happened. Ruth's husband died. Then Orpah's husband died, too. The three women were left alone in the land where Ruth had always lived. Stop.** (Have the child now holding the spool retell this story portion while unwinding some more thread.)

Continue passing the spool. Say: **Naomi told Ruth and Orpah they didn't need to stay with her. So Orpah went back to her own mother's house. Stop.** (Have the child holding the spool retell this story portion and unwind a little more thread.)

Begin passing the spool again. Say: **Ruth could've left Naomi alone. But because the two women were such good friends, Ruth chose to stay with Naomi. The two friends decided to travel back to the land where Naomi had been born. Stop.** (Have the child holding the spool retell this story portion and unwind some thread.)

Pass the spool along. Say: **Ruth and Naomi traveled back to Naomi's old home. But they were hungry and had no food. So Ruth worked hard picking leftover grain to feed them. Ruth gleaned the grain in a field owned by a rich farmer named Boaz. Stop.** (Again, have the child with the spool retell this story portion and unwind some thread.)

Pass the spool and say: **Naomi was happy to hear that Ruth went to Boaz's field to glean grain. Boaz was a kind man and a member of Naomi's family. Then Naomi had a plan.**

She'd help Ruth marry Boaz! Stop. (Have the child with the spool repeat this story portion while unwinding the thread.)

Then pass the thread and say: **Naomi told Ruth to go to Boaz and sleep by his feet. That was a way of asking for Boaz's protection and help. The plan worked! Boaz married Ruth, and they took care of Naomi for the rest of her life. The two loyal friends were together forever. Stop.** (Have the child holding the spool retell this final portion of the story, unwind a little more thread, and hand the spool to you.)

Hold up the spool and ask the following questions:

● **How did Naomi and Ruth help each other?**

● **Why do you suppose Ruth and Naomi were so loyal to each other?**

Say: **When we love someone, we're loyal to them. God wants us to love him and be loyal to him just as we love and are loyal to our friends.**

Pass the spool around the circle once more. Let the children each wind up a portion of the loose thread as they say the names of their best friends.

4. Friendship Bracelets

(You'll need embroidery floss, seed beads, cupcake papers, and scissors.)

Before this activity, cut 8-inch lengths of embroidery floss, being careful not to separate the floss strands. Cut one length for each child and a few extras for any visitors.

Ask kids to find the same partners they had in the Friends Stick Together activity. Tell them to find a place to sit on the floor. Say: **Loyal friends share many things. We're going to share some fun and some work. You and your partner can share in making friendship bracelets to wear.**

Set out cupcake papers with seed beads in them. Hand each child an 8-inch length of embroidery floss. Let one person in each pair get one cupcake paper with beads to share. Tell children to tie a double knot at one end of the floss so the beads won't slip off as they're strung. (You may have to help younger children tie their knots.) Encourage partners to help each other by holding the floss. When they're done stringing beads, have kids tie a double knot at the other end of the floss to hold the beads on. Encourage partners to help each other tie their bracelets onto their wrists.

Say: **Having a loyal friend makes difficult jobs easier. I'm glad we have so many loyal friends in our class!**

5. A Friendship Song

(Before this activity, write the words to the song below on a sheet of newsprint.)

Gather kids into a group to share this new song. Spread out so kids have room to move. Lead the children in singing this song to the tune of "Old MacDonald Had a Farm."

"FRIENDSHIP SONG"

Mr. Boaz had a farm. E-I-E-I-O. And on his farm he cut some wheat. E-I-E-I-O. With a "swish swish" here and a "swash swash" there. (*Swing your arms back and forth as if cutting grain with a scythe.*)
Here a "swish," there a "swash," everywhere a "swish swash." Mr. Boaz had a farm. E-I-E-I-O.

Ruth was gleaning in the field. E-I-E-I-O. Picking grain to make her meal. E-I-E-I-O. With a "pick pick" here and a "pluck pluck" there. (*Bend at the waist and pick up pretend wheat.*)
Here a "pick," there a "pluck," everywhere a "pick pluck." Ruth was gleaning in the field. E-I-E-I-O.

Ruth and Naomi were good friends. E-I-E-I-O. Loyal and caring 'til the end. E-I-E-I-O. With a "hug hug" here and a "pat pat" there. (*Kids give hugs and pats on the back to others who are willing.*)
Here a hug, there a pat, everywhere a "hug pat." Ruth and Naomi were good friends. E-I-E-I-O.

Say: **Singing with friends is fun! We've been learning that good friends are loyal to each other. Because we love God and he's our friend, we want to be loyal to God, too.**

6. Loyal to Others, Loyal to God

(You'll need a Bible and several rolls of Life Savers candy.)

Sit with the kids on the floor. Have a volunteer read aloud Proverbs 18:24b. If you have young children, you may want to read this verse aloud to them. Then say: **God wants us to be loyal to him, to our families, and to our true friends.**

Ask:

● **How can we show loyalty?**

Hold up one piece of Life Savers candy and say: **Loyal friends who love and help us can be real life savers!**

Ask:

● **Who can share a time when a friend was loyal and helped you out?** Allow plenty of time for kids to respond, encouraging everyone to share. If a child isn't able to think of a loyal friend, remind him or her that God is our friend and ask how God has helped.

Give each child three pieces of candy. Say: **Don't eat your candy yet. Find a partner. Take turns holding up a piece of candy and telling one way you can be loyal to God. Then you may eat your first piece of candy. With the next piece, tell one way you can be loyal to a friend. And with the last piece, tell one way you can be loyal to a family member.**

Give kids time to share their ideas and eat their candy. When everyone is finished, say this prayer: **Dear God, we thank you for loyal friends. Please help us see the ways we can be more loyal to you and to our families and friends. In Jesus' name we pray, amen.**

Give children each a hug as they leave.

by Terri Vermillion

8. No Reason for Teasin' (Hannah)

Hannah was the favorite wife of Elkanah. Because Hannah had no children, Elkanah's other wife continually taunted and humiliated her. Hannah learned a lesson our children need to learn—that God is our refuge and always loves us in spite of what others may think or say.

Few of us have missed those fiery darts slung by thoughtless words. Teasing and taunting remarks can be like sharp thorns driven right to the heart. Use this lesson to help children learn what to do if they're teased and remember that God always loves them and comforts them even when people say hurtful things.

A POWERFUL POINT

Though others may hurt our feelings, God loves us.

A LOOK AT THE LESSON

1. Ping-Pong Push Down (6 minutes)
2. Hannah's Last Laugh (6 minutes)
3. Sticks and Stones (6 minutes)
4. Walk a Mile in My Shoes (8 minutes)
5. Super Scope (8 minutes)
6. If Someone Teases You Sometime (5 minutes)

A SPRINKLING OF SUPPLIES

Gather together two Ping-Pong balls, a bucket of water, a Bible, napkins, pretzel sticks, and raisins. You'll also need a pair of men's shoes, a pair of baby shoes, cellophane tape, markers, and newsprint paper.

THE FUN-TO-LEARN LESSON

1. Ping-Pong Push Down

(You'll need a bucket of water and two Ping-Pong balls. Before the activity, carefully poke six to 10 holes in one Ping-Pong ball using the point of a drawing compass, knitting needle, or other sharp object.)

Have the children sit in a circle on the floor. Set the bucket of water in front of you. Hold up the Ping-Pong ball with the holes. Say: **Let's pass this ball around the circle. When you get the ball, say mean, teasing things to it as you poke at the holes with your finger.**

When the Ping-Pong ball has traveled around the circle, say: **Now let's see what happens when we put the ball in water.** Hold the ball under the water until it fills with water and sinks. Let kids see the sunken ball. Ask:

● **How is this sunken ball like how you feel if someone teases you or says hurtful things?**

● **How can we bounce back up when someone tries to push us down with mean words?** Responses may include praying, telling the other person how you feel, ignoring mean words, and asking God to help you forgive the other person.

Say: **A good way to bounce back up is to say, "God loves me." Even when others try to push us down with teasing and mean words, God always loves us. Let's try this: We'll each have a turn at pushing the second Ping-Pong ball under the water. As you let it go, say, "God loves me!"**

Give each child a chance to push the Ping-Pong ball under the water and say, "God loves me" as it pops back up. After every child has had a turn, say: **Sometimes people make fun of us. They try to push us down and make us feel ugly or stupid. You can stay down like the first Ping-Pong ball, or you can say, "God loves me" and bounce back up like the second Ping-Pong ball. God will help you bounce back up and feel good about yourself.**

2. Hannah's Last Laugh

(You'll need a Bible.)

Open your Bible to 1 Samuel 1:1-20. Hold your Bible up, point to it, and say: **The Bible tells a story about a woman named Hannah who was teased a lot.**

Ask:

● **What does it mean to tease and taunt someone?**

Say: **I want to tell you the story of Hannah, but I need your help. Whenever I say the name "Hannah," you're to say, "Ha, ha, Hannah!" Let's try it once: <u>Hannah</u>.** Pause for kids to say, "Ha, ha, Hannah!" **Let's begin our Bible story about <u>Hannah</u>.** Pause for kids' response.

Elkanah was a man who had two wives. One was named Peninnah; the other was named <u>Hannah</u>. Elkanah loved <u>Hannah</u> the best, and that made Peninnah angry and jealous! <u>Hannah</u> had no children. She wished

and wished for a baby. **When other people saw <u>Hannah</u> without children, they teased and taunted her. "You'll never have kids!" Peninnah was the meanest of all. "Ha, ha, <u>Hannah</u>," said Peninnah. "I have children and you don't." The teasing made <u>Hannah</u> feel very sad.**

Ask:

● **Why did Peninnah say mean things to Hannah?**

<u>Hannah's</u> husband, Elkanah, said, "Don't feel sad. I love you best." But Peninnah teased <u>Hannah</u> so often that she made <u>Hannah</u> cry. So <u>Hannah</u> asked God to help.

<u>Hannah</u> knew that God loved her even when others said mean and hurtful things. And God blessed her the next year with a baby boy of her own. When mean old Peninnah tried to tease <u>Hannah</u>, <u>Hannah</u> said, "I don't feel sad. God always loves me, and I can laugh with joy!" And here was her last laugh: (laugh with joy as you say the following words) **Ha-ha-hallelujah! He-he-he loves me!**

Ask:

● **Why was Hannah happy at the end of the story?**

● **How did Hannah deal with teasing and mean words?**

Say: **Hannah knew that God loves us even when others are cruel. When people said mean things, Hannah prayed and asked God for help. Let's say Hannah's last laugh two times to help you remember what to say the next time someone teases you. Ha-ha-hallelujah! He-he-he loves me! Ha-ha-hallelujah! He-he-he loves me!**

3. Sticks and Stones

(You'll need napkins, pretzel sticks, raisins, and a Bible.)

Have the children form pairs and sit

with their partners on the floor. Hand children napkins with pretzel sticks and raisins but tell them not to eat their snacks yet. Say: **Sticks and stones may break my bones, but names can never hurt me.**

Ask:

● **Can mean words hurt us? Why or why not?**

Say: **Mean words won't skin our knees, but they can hurt our feelings. If someone's saying mean things, it sometimes helps to tell that person how we feel. Let's try that. Tell your partner something mean or teasing that someone said to you or someone else. After you've each shared, break a pretzel stick and eat it. Then tell how you could respond. Say, "When you say that, I feel..." and tell your partner how that would make you feel. When you've both told how you feel, eat a raisin.**

Allow time for partners to share, then say: **A good way to deal with teasing is to gently tell that person how we feel.**

Open the Bible to Ephesians 4:29 and have a volunteer read it aloud. Ask:

● **Why is it important to say what people need?**

Say: **Mean words may hurt our feelings. But words that are encouraging and kind make us feel better. God wants us to love others. Before you eat the rest of your sticks and stones, let's pray.**

Dear God, please help us learn how to handle unkind words. Let us share our feelings and turn to you for help. We know that even when others tease us, you love us. In Jesus' name, amen.

As children enjoy their snacks, say: **Saying kind words to people who tease us is a way to show God's love.**

Let's see how being sensitive to other people helps, too.

4. Walk a Mile in My Shoes

(You'll need a pair of men's shoes and a pair of baby shoes.)

Say: **There's a phrase that says, "You should never judge people until you've walked a mile in their shoes."**

Ask:

● **What does it mean to walk in someone else's shoes?**

Say: **Today we'll play a game that will help us understand people instead of judging or teasing them. In this game, you'll get a chance to race in someone else's shoes.**

Have children form four teams and line up at one end of the room. Give the first child on each team one shoe. Tell those children to put the shoes on as best they can.

Say: **When I say, "go," you'll hop on that shoe to the opposite end of the room and back. Then give your shoe to the next person on your team.**

When everyone is finished, have children sit in a circle on the floor. Ask:

● **How can walking in someone else's shoes help us understand how they feel?**

● **Why is it important to try to understand how others feel?**

● **What do you wish people understood about you or the way you feel?**

Say: **When we've been in someone else's place, we're more sensitive to their feelings. God wants us to love all people and treat them with love and kindness.**

5. Super Scopes

(You'll need a Bible, a sheet of newsprint for each child, cellophane tape, and markers.)

Hold the Bible up and say: **Let's read what the Bible says about how God sees us.** Read aloud 1 Samuel 16:7c. Then ask:

● **What part of us does God look at?**

Say: **Today we're going to make "super scopes" to help us remember that God sees our hearts. He loves us just as we are. God wants us to look at others through his eyes, too.**

Give children each a sheet of newsprint. Tell them to decorate the paper with colorful markers. With the colored side out, show kids how to roll the paper into a long cone shape. Have children help each other tape the sides of their cones to keep them from unrolling.

When everyone has finished, say: **Let's use our super scopes to look at others the way God looks at them.** Help the children form two concentric circles with circles facing each other.

Say: **When I turn the lights off, begin walking in a circle. When I turn the lights on, stop and look through your super scope at the person across from you. As you do this, tell that person a good thing about himself or herself.** Continue until you've allowed the children to affirm each other three times.

6. If Someone Teases You Sometime

(Before you begin this activity, write the words to the song below on newsprint.)

"IF SOMEONE TEASES YOU SOMETIME"

(to the tune of "London Bridge")

**If someone teases you today,
you can pray or
turn away.
Or you can tell them how you feel;
that's God's way.**

**If someone's mean in what they say,
you can pray or
turn away.
Or you can tell them how you feel;
that's God's way.**

Say: **Today we've talked about teasing and how God loves us even when others say mean things. We've learned different ways God helps us handle teasing. We can choose to pray like Hannah did. Or sometimes it's best to tell someone how teasing makes us feel. Let's learn a new song to remind us what to do when we're teased.**

Show children the lyrics you've written out and lead them in singing the song. For older children, add actions. As each syllable is sung, touch your head, shoulders, knees, and toes and keep repeating in rhythm throughout the song. For real excitement, speed up your singing and the accompanying actions with each verse!

by Ellen Javernick

9. Listen Up!
(Samuel)

"And then God told me..." That's a statement that stumps many adults. For children, it's even more puzzling. How does anyone "hear" God speak? In the Bible, the young Samuel wondered the same thing. Was it really God speaking to him in the night?

In our busy society, time to pause and listen is often considered a luxury. But for those of us who follow God, those quiet moments may be the most important part of our day. Use this lesson to help children learn that God can and will speak to us if we are willing to listen carefully.

A POWERFUL POINT

We can learn to listen to God.

A LOOK AT THE LESSON

1. Lend an Ear (7 minutes)
2. Whisperphone (9 minutes)
3. Wake-Up Call (8 minutes)
4. Listen Up! (8 minutes)
5. Elephant Ears (9 minutes)
6. Silent Speaking (7 minutes)

A SPRINKLING OF SUPPLIES

Gather a Bible, a cassette player, a musical cassette tape, a toy telephone, poster board, markers, scissors, glue, and photocopies of the "Samuel Listens" handout (p. 49). You'll also need soft margarine, cinnamon-sugar, a spoon, plastic knives, and one flour tortilla for each child.

THE FUN-TO-LEARN LESSON

1. Lend an Ear

(You'll need a cassette player and musical cassette tape.)

As kids arrive, play a musical cassette tape loudly. Speak in a soft voice and tell the children you're very glad they've come today. Spend a few moments telling how each child is special and important to your class. Make sure the volume of the music drowns out your voice.

After a few minutes, turn off the music. Gather the children in a circle and ask:

● **Did you like what I said to each of you? Explain.**

● **Why did you have a problem hearing me?**

● **When is it important to listen carefully?**

Say: **Sometimes we have to listen very carefully to hear what's being said, like when you're getting instructions for homework or when your parents tell you what you can have for a snack. Today we're going to learn about listening to God. We want to be careful listeners to God and not let other things like the loud music I just played keep us from paying attention.**

2. Whisperphone

(You'll need a toy telephone and a Bible.)

Sit with kids in a circle and say: **Let's play a game called Whisperphone. It'll help us practice careful listening. I'll put this telephone receiver next** to my neighbor's ear and whisper a message into it. Then I'll hand the telephone to my neighbor, and he or she will whisper the message to the next person. You'll have to listen carefully because the message can't be repeated. When the telephone has traveled around the circle, the last person may repeat the message out loud.

Whisper the following message to the child on your right: "God wants us to listen carefully to him." When the message and telephone have been sent around the circle, ask the last child to repeat the message aloud.

If the message is repeated correctly, ask:

● **Why were we able to pass the message correctly?**

If the last person restates the message incorrectly, ask:

● **Why did our message get mixed up?**

● **What can happen if we don't listen carefully or if we don't listen to the right person?**

● **Who can tell about a time he or she listened to the wrong person or didn't get a message right?**

Say: **We want to pay special attention to the messages God gives us.**

Ask:

● **What are some ways we can listen to God?** (Answers may include by reading the Bible, through prayer, or by listening in Sunday school.)

Say: **Reading the Bible is a wonderful way to learn about and listen to God. Now let's act out a story from the Bible about a boy who listened to God in a different way.**

3. Wake-Up Call

(You'll need a Bible.)

Sit with the children on the floor. Open the Bible to 1 Samuel 3:1-20 and say: **Our Bible story is about a boy named Samuel. Let's act out the story together. Watch me and do what I do.**

Samuel was a young boy who lived with an old man named Eli. Eli was a priest. Fold your hands in prayer. **Samuel's mother sent Samuel to live with Eli to learn about serving God. So Eli and young Samuel lived together in a church, and they both loved God very much.**

One night, Eli and Samuel fell fast asleep. Lie down on the floor. **You may find a place to sleep now, too.** Pause for kids to pick sleeping spaces and lie down. Very quietly say: **When you hear me call the name "Samuel," run to me and say, "Here I am!"**

As he slept, Samuel heard someone calling his name. "Samuel..." Pause while the children run to you and say, "Here I am!" Then reply by saying: **I didn't call you. Go back and lie down.** When the children are lying down again, softly say: **Samuel...** Wait for the children to run to you, then say: **I didn't call. Go back and lie down.** After the children are lying down, say: **Samuel!**

When the children run over to you, ask:

● **Who do you think was calling Samuel?**

Say: **Samuel didn't know it was God who was talking, but Eli knew. So Eli told Samuel, "The Lord is calling you. Go back and lie down. If God calls again, say, 'Speak, Lord. I am your servant and I am listening.' "** Give the children time to lie down. Then say: **Samuel!**

Help the children say, "Speak, Lord. I am your servant and I am listening." Then say: **And Samuel listened to God.**

God told Samuel that Eli would be **punished because Eli's sons had done bad things and Eli hadn't stopped them. After Samuel heard what God had to say, Samuel lay down and slept until morning.** Have the kids lie down and pretend to sleep.

In the morning, Samuel woke up. Yawn and stretch your arms. **Eli came to Samuel and asked, "What did God tell you?"**

Ask:

● **What was God's message?**

● **How do think Samuel felt about telling Eli what God said?**

Say: **Even though Samuel was afraid to tell Eli, he was obedient and told Eli all God had said. Eli knew God was right. And because Samuel listened to God, God blessed Samuel as he grew up.**

Gather the children in a circle on the floor and ask:

● **Why do you think God spoke to Samuel?**

● **Do you think God speaks to you? Explain.**

Say: **God wants us to listen to him, just as Samuel did. Let's find out how we can be good listeners.**

4. Listen Up!

(You'll need poster board, markers, glue, scissors, and a photocopy of the "Samuel Listens" handout on page 49 for each child.)

Say: **Find a partner, and we'll see how good you are at listening to directions.** Give each child a handout. **We're going to make puzzles from these pictures of Samuel listening to God's voice. First color the picture, then glue it to a piece of poster board and cut out the puzzle pieces.**

Allow time for the children to finish making their puzzles. Circulate and af-

firm partners who are following directions well. When kids have all finished their puzzles, say: **Now let's try something fun. Give directions for your partner to put the puzzle together with his or her eyes closed. Decide which of you will give directions first; then we'll switch.** After one minute, have partners switch roles. When each child has been the direction giver and follower, ask:

● **What was it like to do the puzzle with your eyes closed?**

● **How closely did you listen to your partner?**

● **How was listening to your partner like listening to God? How was it different?**

Say: **It's important to listen carefully because we may miss directions or information we need to keep us safe and happy. We can use our ears and our hearts to listen to God. I'm glad we don't need ears as big as elephants' ears to listen to God! Shall we have some fun with ears we can eat?**

5. Elephant Ears

(You'll need soft margarine, cinnamon-sugar, a spoon, plastic knives, and one flour tortilla for each child.)

Say: **We've been learning about listening to God. I have a riddle for you about some very large ears. See if you can guess whose ears I'm talking about:**

We're wrinkly and lumpy and have small, gray heads,

and our ears are as large as pillows on beds!

Who are we? (Elephants!)

Pause for kids to guess. Then say: **Let's make a snack to remind us of how important it is to listen to God. We'll make ears like the animal with** the biggest ears—elephants!

Give each child a tortilla. Let the kids use plastic knives to spread margarine on tortillas then sprinkle cinnamon-sugar over the margarine. Show them how to fold the tortillas in half to make elephant ears. If you have a microwave close by, heat the tortillas for about ten seconds. Then let kids enjoy eating the elephant ears.

6. Silent Speaking

Say: **Did you know that we can listen when we pray? We usually think of praying as** *talking* **to God. Today when we pray, we'll try** *listening* **to God. I'll pray, and then we'll quietly listen for God to speak to our hearts.**

Pray: **Dear God, we're so glad you love us and want to speak to us. Please teach us new ways to listen to you more carefully. Help make our hearts still and quiet so we can hear you better.**

Allow about one minute of silence before saying: **In Jesus' name, amen.** Then invite children to share what they thought and felt as they listened.

by Christine Yount

SAMUEL LISTENS

Directions: Color the picture. Glue this page to poster board or cardboard. Cut along the lines to make a puzzle.

10. Promises, Promises (David)

The Bible tells us that God always keeps his word and wants us to honor the promises we make, too. One of the best examples of biblical promises is the story of David and Jonathan's friendship. Their promise of loyal friendship was honored and kept even after Jonathan's death. The two friends knew that the value of a promise lies in honoring it.

Children hear all kinds of promises and learn quickly that many promises aren't kept. It's easy for children to get the idea that promises are more suggestions of what we might do rather than vows to be honored. Use this lesson to help children understand the importance of keeping promises and that God's promises can always be trusted.

A POWERFUL POINT

It's important to keep our promises.

A LOOK AT THE LESSON

1. Precious Promises (9 minutes)
2. Two of a Kind (8 minutes)
3. David and Jonathan's Promise (8 minutes)
4. Standing on a Promise (7 minutes)
5. Promises From the Heart (8 minutes)
6. Firm and Fast (5 minutes)

A SPRINKLING OF SUPPLIES

Gather a Bible, paper towels, white paper, cereal, glue, markers or crayons, scissors, and magazines. You'll also need a raw egg and a small plastic bowl for every pair of children.

THE FUN-TO-LEARN LESSON

1. Precious Promises

(For each pair of children, you'll need a small plastic or paper bowl, a raw egg, and three paper towels.)

Have children form pairs. Hand each pair a small plastic or paper bowl, a raw egg, and three paper towels. Say: **Today we're going to talk about promises. Let's start by having some messy fun. Set your bowl on the floor on top of your paper towels. Kneel over your bowl, then you and your partner can help hold the egg over the bowl. We'll recite "Humpty Dumpty," and when we say, "Humpty Dumpty had a great fall," let the egg drop into the bowl.**

Recite "Humpty Dumpty." When everyone's egg is broken, ask:
- **What happened to your egg?**
- **What does your broken egg remind you of?**
- **How does it feel when someone breaks a promise?**
- **Do you think you and your partner can put the egg back together?**

Allow a few moments for children to try to mend their eggs. Have the kids wipe their hands on the paper towels, then throw away the towels. Set the bowls and eggs aside.

Say: **When we break a promise, it can't be made new again. God always keeps his promises from breaking, and he wants us keep our promises from breaking, too. Today we'll hear a story about a special promise that nothing could break. Now let's each pretend we're Humpty Dumpty and act out the rhyme as we say it again.**

Repeat the rhyme and act out motions such as sitting on a wall, falling off of the wall, and lying on the ground. When you've repeated the action rhyme a few times, say: **God wants us to be careful to keep the promises we make. This means we have to make wise promises. Let's look at some wise and foolish promises.**

2. Two of a Kind

(You'll need cereal, paper towels, magazines, white paper, scissors, and glue. Before this activity, cut out a magazine advertisement for any sweetened cereal. If possible, find an ad that matches the cereal you're going to use for this activity.)

Ask:

● **What are some ads you've seen in magazines, in newspapers, or on television?**

● **What are some of the good things they promise?** (Some responses may include good taste, lots of fun, it doesn't cost much, or it will make you prettier.)

Say: **Some promises are good promises. A good promise is one that's kept. But some promises are poor promises. A poor promise is one that's not kept. Let's get into small groups and see if you can pick out good promises and poor promises.**

Form small groups of two or three children. Pass each group a magazine and a sheet of paper. They'll also need scissors and glue. Say: **Your group will decide on an ad to cut out and glue on your paper. Then have your group decide what you think is being promised in the ad. Talk about whether you think it's a good promise or a poor promise and why.**

Allow time for groups to finish gluing and talking about their ads. Then flip the light switch a few times to get their attention. Say: **Let's put our things away and talk about what you've found.** Have each group stand and display its paper. Ask each group the following questions:

● **What was being promised in your ad?**

● **Was it a good or poor promise? Explain.**

Say: **Promises that aren't kept make people feel bad.** Hold up the cereal ad you cut out. **This ad promises good taste. Let's see if that was a good promise.**

Give each child a paper towel and a handful of sweetened cereal. When everyone has tasted the cereal, ask:

● **Did the cereal keep the promise of good taste?**

Pause for responses. Then say: **Just like this cereal tastes sweet, promises that are kept are sweet. I'm going to tell you a Bible story about a sweet promise that was made between two good friends.**

3. David and Jonathan's Promise

(You'll need a Bible.)

Seat children in a circle. Open the Bible to 2 Samuel 9. Hold up the Bible. Point to it and say: **Our Bible story today is about a promise between two friends and how they kept their** promise forever. You can help me tell the story. We'll pass around the Bible as I tell you the story. When I say "stop," the person holding the Bible will say, "A promise made by a friend is a promise kept to the end." Let's say that together. Practice repeating the rhyme until the children are comfortable with the words.

Begin passing the Bible and say: **David and Jonathan were best friends. David loved Jonathan like a brother, and the two young men promised they'd be friends forever. Stop.** (Have the child holding the Bible repeat the rhyme, then continue passing the Bible.)

Jonathan's father was King Saul. King Saul was afraid David would take over as king because David was strong and wise and brave. King Saul was jealous of David and wanted to kill him. But even this didn't break David and Jonathan's promise of friendship. Stop. (Have the child holding the Bible repeat the rhyme, then continue passing the Bible.)

Jonathan told David that his father was planning to hurt David. David decided to leave. And again Jonathan and David promised they'd always be friends. Stop. (Have the child holding the Bible repeat the rhyme, then continue passing the Bible.)

David and Jonathan didn't see each other for a long time. But even though they were far apart, they remained friends. Stop. (Have the child holding the Bible repeat the rhyme, then continue passing the Bible.)

When David returned to Jonathan's land, both Jonathan and King Saul were dead. David missed his friend, but even death didn't break the promise they'd made to be friends forever. Stop. (Have the child holding the Bible repeat the rhyme, then

continue passing the Bible.)

When David became the new king, Jonathan's son came to King David for help. David remembered his promise and welcomed Jonathan's son as a friend. David's promise of loyalty and friendship with Jonathan was kept forever. Stop. (Have the child holding the Bible repeat the rhyme.)

Ask:

● **What was David and Jonathan's promise to each other?**

● **Do you think it was a good promise? Why or why not?**

● **Why do you suppose David and Jonathan kept their promise of friendship even through hard times?**

Say: **Because David and Jonathan cared for each other so much, their promise was never broken. Let's repeat the rhyme one more time together to remind us how important it is to keep our promises: "A promise made by a friend is a promise kept to the end."**

4. Standing on a Promise

(You'll need a Bible and paper.)

Have the children each find a partner, then hand each person a sheet of paper. Say: **Now we're going to practice standing on a promise. Stand beside your partner. Each of you may stand on your piece of paper. Now try to pull your partner's paper out from under his or her feet.** Give the kids time to tug on their partners' papers. Then ask:

● **Why can't the paper be moved?**

Say: **When we stand on a promise, it can't be moved either. When we stand on a promise, it means we'll do what we promised. When we stand on a promise, we're like David when he kept his promise to Jon-**

athan. Sit on your paper and let's see what the Bible says about promises that God makes.

Open the Bible to 1 Kings 8:20a and read it aloud. Ask:

● **Why do you suppose God keeps his promises?**

● **How does it make you feel to know that God always keeps his promises?**

● **How do you suppose God feels when we keep our promises?**

Say: **Let's play a game to remind us how important it is to stand on our promises. We'll pretend our papers are promises. You'll line up at one end of the room, and I'll be "It." When I say "go," you'll run to the other end of the room. I'll try to tag you, but if you put your promise down, stand on it, and say, "You promised I'd be safe" before I touch you, you'll be safe! If I catch you before you stand on your promise, you must help me tag the others!**

When children safely reach the other side of the room, say "go" again and have them run back as you try to tag them. Continue until everyone is caught. When the game is over, have the children sit on their papers. Ask:

● **Why did having a promise to stand on make the game easier?**

Say: **When we stand on our promises, we show others they can trust us to help them and love them. Keeping promises is important!**

5. Promises From the Heart

(You'll need markers or crayons and paper.)

Direct kids to sit at tables. Say: **When we keep promises, it shows we care about keeping our word. When we keep promises to our friends, it's because we love them and want to do**

as we said we would. **Let's draw a picture of a promise you have kept or could make and keep to a special friend.**

Give children time to draw their pictures. While they're working, circulate and ask questions such as "How can God help you keep promises?" and "Why is it important to keep promises made to God?"

When everyone is finished, say: **Let's get into groups of three or four, and you can each tell about the picture you drew and what promise you made or kept. After you've had a chance to share, sit on your paper.** Continue until you see everyone sitting on his or her paper. Then ask kids to put their pictures on the table to take home later.

6. Firm and Fast

Assign each child a partner and have them stand facing each other. Say: **A promise is always made between at least two people. David made Jonathan a promise. God makes each of us promises. Let's face our partners and act out a rhyme to let each other know how important it is to keep our promises. I'll say the rhyme once and do the actions. Then we'll say the words and do the actions together.** Clap on the underlined words.

I'm going to <u>stand</u>
(*Step your right foot forward.*)
on my <u>promises</u> <u>firm</u> and <u>fast</u>;
(*Step your left foot forward.*)
my <u>word</u> of <u>honor</u> is <u>made</u> to <u>last</u>!
(*Turn around in place.*)

I'm going to <u>hop</u>
(*Hop in place on your right foot.*)
to my <u>promises</u> <u>firm</u> and <u>fast</u>;
(*Hop in place on your left foot.*)

my <u>word</u> of <u>honor</u> is <u>made</u> to <u>last</u>!
(Hop around in place.)

I'm going to <u>dance</u>
(Dance in place.)
on my <u>promises</u> <u>firm</u> and <u>fast</u>;
(Dance in place.)
my <u>word</u> of <u>honor</u> is <u>made</u> to <u>last</u>!
(Turn around in place.)

You may wish to add actions like "nod to my promises" and "sit on my promises." If time allows, have children invent other actions and words to use.

Ask kids to sit with their partners where they are. Say: **Take hold of your partner's hands and let's say a prayer. Dear God, thank you for your promises. We know you always keep your word. Help us make and keep wise promises, too. In Jesus' name, amen.**

by Terri Vermillion

11. Partners in Peace (Abigail)

The biblical peacemaker Abigail provides a good example of the positive effects of making peace instead of war. Abigail stepped into the middle of a fight and offered a peaceful settlement that averted death and destruction.

Nearly every day we hear about gang fights, murders, and wars around the world. And children experience disagreements, fights, and arguments with siblings and classmates. It's important for our kids to learn how to find peaceful solutions to difficult problems. Use this lesson to teach children ways to get along with others peacefully and to solve problems with love instead of anger.

A POWERFUL POINT

We can learn how to settle conflicts peacefully.

A LOOK AT THE LESSON

1. Spat Chat (8 minutes)
2. Broken Hearts (7 minutes)
3. Mended Hearts (7 minutes)
4. Abigail, Abigail! (8 minutes)
5. Have-a-Heart Relay (8 minutes)
6. Peace Partners (7 minutes)

A SPRINKLING OF SUPPLIES

You'll need a Bible; icing; plastic knives; a black marker; red construction paper; cellophane tape; four plastic bandages; a large, heart-shaped cookie; a cookie sheet or pizza pan; and a photocopy of the "Spat Chat" handout (p. 59).

THE FUN-TO-LEARN LESSON

1. Spat Chat

(You'll need one photocopy of the "Spat Chat" handout on page 59.)

Before this activity, cut out the cards from the handout. Sit with the children in a circle on the floor. Say: **Today we're going to talk about what happens when we fight or argue with others, and we'll learn ways to settle disagreements peacefully.**

Have children form pairs. When everyone has a partner, say: **One set of partners will come up and choose a card. I'll read the card out loud so the class can hear. Then those partners will act out the disagreement or fight that's on the card. When I say "stop," the rest of us will brainstorm ways to settle that disagreement peacefully.**

As the class brainstorms ideas for peaceful answers, lead them to consider these answers: talking it over, laughing, taking a walk, or asking forgiveness.

When everyone who wishes to has had a chance to role play, say: **Fighting and arguing in real life make us feel awful. It's important to settle disagreements and fights without hurting yourself or someone else. When we settle our problems peacefully, feelings don't get hurt as badly. Let's look at what fighting does to our feelings.**

2. Broken Hearts

(Before this activity, bake a large, heart-shaped cookie using refrigerated sugar-cookie dough. You'll also need a cookie sheet or pizza pan.)

Seat children with you on the floor. Place the heart-shaped cookie on a cookie sheet or pizza pan in the center of the circle.

Say: **When we argue and fight, feelings get hurt. Fighting makes us feel bad. Let's go around the circle and each tell about a fight we had with someone. Don't say any names but tell how you felt when your feelings or another person's were hurt. When you tell about how you felt, break off a piece of the heart cookie in the center of the circle. Hold on to the piece of cookie.**

After everyone's had a turn to share, say: **A heart is a very breakable thing. We can break a heart easily if we're unkind or if we fight with others. We want to be careful with other people's hearts and feelings. And we want to be careful with our own, too. Let's talk about how to help when feelings are hurt.**

3. Mended Hearts

(You'll need icing and plastic knives.) Ask:

● **Who can tell about a time he or she or someone else stopped a fight?**

● **How was it stopped?** (Some responses may include "they stepped between us," "asked us to talk it over," "put us in 'time out' to cool off," or "sent me to my room.")

Say: **A person who helps stop an argument or fight is called a peacemaker. Peacemakers make peace between people who are disagreeing. Peacemakers help mend broken hearts and hurt feelings. Let's be peacemakers and work together to mend the broken-heart cookie with this icing.**

Have the children work together to put the pieces of the heart cookie back together. Spread icing on the pieces to hold them together. When the cookie is complete, say: **Fighting or arguing only makes a disagreement worse. We want to learn how to settle disagreements peacefully and with love. I'd like to tell you a Bible story about a woman who was a peacemaker.** Allow children to choose a piece of the heart cookie to eat.

4. Abigail, Abigail!

(You'll need a Bible, red construction paper, tape, four plastic bandages, and a black marker. Before this activity, cut out a large, red heart from the construction paper. Tape the heart to a wall. Print one of the following letters on each bandage: L, O, V, and E.)

Gather kids in a group near the heart you taped to the wall. Open the Bible to 1 Samuel 25. Say: **Our Bible story is about a woman who learned how important it is to settle fights peacefully. The woman's name was Abigail, and Abigail was a peacemaker. You can help me tell the story.** Pass the bandages to four children and hand another child the black marker.

As I tell the Bible story, you'll draw cracks on the heart on the wall to show how fighting hurts us. Then we'll see how Abigail helped mend those cracks.

Abigail was married to a mean man named Nabal. Nabal was rich, but he was very stingy, too. Nabal didn't want to share his riches with anyone. (Have the child with the marker draw a small crack across the heart and hand the marker to another child.)

Before David was king, he and his soldiers camped out, and they were hungry and thirsty. David knew Nabal was nearby. So he sent 10 of his men to go to Nabal and ask for food and water. But Nabal was rude. He said, "Who is this David? I won't give him any of my food or water!" (Have the child with the marker draw a small crack across the heart and hand the marker to another child.)

The men returned and told David how mean and rude Nabal had been. David became angry and decided to get even with Nabal. David wanted to kill Nabal and his men. (Have the child with the marker draw a small crack across the heart and hand the marker to another child.)

When Nabal's wife, Abigail, found out what had happened, it made her feel awful. (Have someone draw a final crack across the heart. Then have that child hand the marker to you.)

Abigail wanted to make peace between David and her husband. So she gathered up lots of food and water to take to David and his men. She went to David's camp and said, "I'm sorry for the mean way my husband acted." (Tell a child with a bandage to place it on a crack on the heart. It doesn't matter which letter is on the bandage.)

Abigail said, "Nabal was cruel and selfish. I ask your forgiveness." (Call on another child to place a second bandage over a crack on the heart.)

Abigail said, "I hope you'll accept the food and water I've brought as a gift. I hope that you'll forgive us." (Have a child place the third bandage over a crack on the heart.)

After Abigail asked forgiveness and made peace, David felt better. He knew he would have done an awful thing to kill Nabal and his men. He thanked Abigail for her kindness and said he wouldn't hurt Nabal or any of his men. (Have a child place the last bandage on the last crack.)

Ask:

● **Why did Abigail want to make peace?**

● **Do you think she was a good peacemaker? Explain.**

● **What do you suppose might've happened if Abigail hadn't been a peacemaker?**

Point to the heart and ask:

● **What do the letters on the bandages spell?**

Point to the letters as the children spell out the word "love." Say: **Fighting and arguing make us feel awful. It's important to know how to settle a disagreement without feeling hurt or hurting someone else. When we settle fights peacefully, we offer love instead of hurt.**

5. Have-a-Heart Relay

(You'll need red construction paper and cellophane tape. Before you begin this activity, cut out two 6-inch hearts. Cut each heart into six puzzle pieces.)

Place each set of puzzle pieces in a pile at one end of the room by a wall. Set the tape between the piles. Have children form two groups and line up at the other end of the room opposite the puzzle pieces.

Say: **Abigail hurried to mend hurt feelings between David and Nabal. Let's see how quickly we can mend a heart. When I say "go," the first person in each line will hop on one foot to the pile of puzzle pieces. Choose a puzzle piece and tape it on the wall. Then hop back and tap the next per-**

son in line. **That person will hop to the puzzle pieces and add another piece of the heart and so on. We'll see if both groups can mend a heart and be peacemakers.**

After the game, have kids sit in a circle on the floor. Say: **You did wonderfully well mending those hearts. But God is the only one who truly mends broken hearts. We can help by being peacemakers. When we help prevent or stop a fight, God works to mend hearts with love!**

6. Peace Partners

(You'll need a Bible.)

Hold up the Bible and say: **God knows how important it is for us to act peacefully. Let's read what the Bible says about being God's peacemakers.** Open the Bible to Matthew 5:9 and read it aloud.

Ask:

● **What will the peacemakers be called?**

Say: **When we're peacemakers, God calls us his children. That's very special and shows how much God loves us. Turn to the person next to you and tell that person you're glad he or she can be a peacemaker this week.**

After a few moments, say: **Join hands and let's say a prayer asking God to help us be peacemakers. Dear God, thank you for teaching us about being peacemakers. Please help us learn to settle disagreements with love and understanding. In Jesus' name, amen.**

by Christine Yount

SPAT CHAT

Directions: Photocopy this handout and cut out the cards. Have children act out the disagreements described. Then brainstorm ways to settle the conflict peacefully.

CARD 1

You're at school. A girl grabs your math paper and tears it in half. Now you're angry at her.

CARD 2

At home, you and your brother get into a fight over whose night it is to do the dishes.

CARD 3

You're playing a game, and you and your friend argue about whose turn it is to play next.

CARD 4

Your teacher thinks you were running down the hall, and you disagree with her.

CARD 5

Your friend has made you late to a party, but your friend says it was your own fault you were late.

CARD 6

Your new sweater is missing. The last time you saw it, your sister was wearing it. Now you're arguing over the missing sweater.

CARD 7

You get into a disagreement with your neighbor about last night's soccer score.

CARD 8

You've been playing baseball and just slid into home plate. You thought you were safe, but the umpire says you're out. Neither of you can agree, and you both become angry.

12. Following God (Josiah)

King Josiah is a powerful example of someone's choosing to follow God with total commitment. God ordered Josiah to clean out and destroy the pagan temples that Josiah's forefathers had built. Even when complying with God's commands meant hard work and tough decisions, King Josiah willingly chose to follow his divine leader.

One childhood game everyone enjoys playing is Follow the Leader. Children love to follow anywhere the leader takes them—up and down and all around. But following God is more important than a game. Children need to learn how important it is to listen to God and then obey him. Use this lesson to teach children that God is the only leader to follow.

A POWERFUL POINT

It's important to obey God.

A LOOK AT THE LESSON

1. What a Mess! (7 minutes)
2. Josiah's Job (9 minutes)
3. Follow the Leader (9 minutes)
4. Delicious Directions (8 minutes)
5. Follow in His Footsteps (8 minutes)
6. Pray to Obey (5 minutes)

A SPRINKLING OF SUPPLIES

Gather a Bible, newspapers, a wastebasket, black construction paper, scissors, masking tape, pencils, a bag of small marshmallows, a box of toothpicks, paper towels, poster board, and markers.

THE FUN-TO-LEARN LESSON

1. What a Mess!

(You'll need newspapers. Before the children arrive, mess up their classroom. Toss newspapers around the room, scatter books on the floor, and turn over a few chairs or a table.)

As children arrive, tell them they need to straighten up the room before class begins. When the room is clean, sit with the children on the floor and ask:

● **What was it like to clean up someone else's mess?**

● **What made you choose to clean it up?** (Answers may include "You told us to," "I wanted to clean our room," or "I don't like messes.")

Say: **When something is dirty, it isn't as nice as something clean. All of you worked hard and did a fine job when I asked you to clean up the room. You obeyed, and our room looks much better now. Today we're going to hear a story about a young king who had to clean house—God's house.**

2. Josiah's Job

(You'll need a Bible, a wastebasket, and the newspapers from the previous activity.)

Have the children each crumple a few newspapers. Make a pile of the newspapers in the center of the floor. Then have the children sit in a circle around the pile of papers. Set a wastebasket at one end of the room.

Point to the pile of papers and say:

A long time ago, God's temple on earth was dirty and needed cleaning. God's house was dirty because people had put idols in it.

Ask:

● Who can tell us what an idol is?

Say: **An idol isn't a real god. It's a thing people make and worship instead of God.** Open the Bible to 2 Kings 22 and 23. **Our Bible story is about a young king named Josiah. You can help me tell the story. Whenever I say the words "clean" or "cleaned," I'll point to two people to go to the pile and grab a crumpled paper wad. Then they'll run to the wastebasket and toss the trash away.**

Read the story below, pausing after each underlined word.

Josiah was a young king who loved and obeyed God. God saw that King Josiah's heart was pure and clean (point to two children). **God also saw there were idols in his temple and knew his temple wasn't clean** (point to two children). **King Josiah knew it was wrong to worship idols. He knew God was the only one to worship and follow. King Josiah wanted to obey God and make God's temple clean** (point to two children).

King Josiah tossed out the idols. He smashed them to pieces. King Josiah destroyed everything that wasn't clean (point to two children) **in God's house. For years Josiah traveled to temples of false gods and threw out the idols that people had set up. Then King Josiah told his people to worship and follow only God. And King Josiah told them to keep God's house pure and clean** (point to two children).

Ask:

● **Why do you think Josiah chose to obey God?**

● **Why is it wise for us to obey God?**

Say: **King Josiah obeyed God because he loved God. Following God and obeying him are good ways of telling God we love him and want only God to be our leader.**

3. Follow the Leader

(You'll need black construction paper, scissors, pencils, and masking tape.)

Have children form pairs, then hand each child a sheet of black construction paper. Say: **Josiah followed in God's footsteps. Let's see how easy it is to follow in someone else's footsteps. Help each other trace one of your feet on your black paper. Then both of you will cut out your footprints. Don't write your name on the footprint.**

When all the footprints have been made, gather the children in a circle. Hand each child a small piece of masking tape. Say: **Bend down and tape your footprint to the floor. You may place it in any direction you wish. Now let's see what it's like to follow in someone's footsteps.**

Let the children walk around the circle, stepping on the footprints. Encourage them to step exactly on top of each print. For real excitement and challenge, choose a child to be the leader and do one or more of the following: speed up the walking pace, add clapping or hopping motions, walk backward, or hop on one foot around the footprints. Switch leaders until everyone's had a turn. Then tell the children to carefully untape the footprints they're on and hand them to you. Set the footprints aside until later.

Have the kids sit in a circle on the floor. Ask:

● **Who did we follow in this game?**

● **How was this game like following God?**

● **Why isn't it always easy to follow and obey God?**

Say: **God wants us to obey and follow him. It may not always be easy, like Josiah found out, but it's important to follow God and listen carefully for his directions. Let's find out what happens when we don't listen and obey well.**

4. Delicious Directions

(You'll need a bag of small marshmallows, paper towels, and a box of toothpicks.)

Form three groups. Hand each group a paper towel with a handful of toothpicks and marshmallows. Say: **Let's see how well you listen and follow directions. Choose a person in your group to be the director. The other people in your group will be followers. I'll secretly tell the directors what your group is to construct. When I say "build," you'll have one minute to follow the directions your director gives you. Work together and listen carefully!**

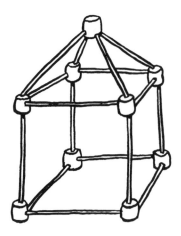

Show the director in each group the sketch of the church on this page. Tell directors to give directions aloud to their groups so the buildings turn out like the sketch. The directors may not touch the buildings.

When one minute is up, flip the lights off and on to get the children's attention. Tell children to join you in a circle on the floor. Have each group display its building. Then show the children the sketch. Ask:

● **How did your building turn out?**

● **What made the directions easy or difficult?**

● **What can happen if we don't listen carefully to directions?**

● **Why is it important to listen to God?**

Say: **We want to listen to God and follow him just like King Josiah. When we listen carefully, we'll be sure to do what God desires.**

Share the rest of the marshmallows and ask children to tell about times they didn't listen well to someone and what happened.

5. Follow in His Footsteps

(You'll need a Bible, markers, scissors, masking tape, and poster board. Before this activity, use the poster board to make five footprints. Make each footprint about 2 feet long. On one footprint write, "I want to follow in your footsteps, God!" Tape this footprint to a wall and set the markers beneath it.)

Have the children sit with you on the floor. Hold up the Bible and say: **I want to read what the Bible says about how Josiah obeyed God.** Read 2 Kings 22:2 aloud.

Then say: **King Josiah never stopped doing what was right and never stopped obeying God. This is how God wants us to be. When we** ask God to help us follow him, we want to obey God's leading. Let's play a game about asking God to help us be better followers.

Form two groups with the children. Have the kids in each group stand close behind each other in a line. Hand each group two footprints. Tell children to stand on their groups' footprints, and you'll tape all their feet to the paper footprints. When you've taped all the children's feet in each group to the two footprints, say: **When I say "go," you'll all walk together on your footprints to the foot on the wall. Sign your name on the footprint. When each person in your group has signed his or her name, walk back to the starting place.**

Walking this way is a challenge! If your kids are having trouble getting started, tell them to count, "One, two, one, two." On the count of one, step with your right foot; on the count of two, step with your left foot.

After kids have all signed their names, let them untape their feet. Ask:

● **What are some ways to follow and obey God?** (Encourage the children to include answers such as reading the Bible, praying, and going to church.)

Say: **Like Josiah, we want to obey God and follow him. Being willing to follow God will help us be more obedient even during the times it may be hard to follow.**

6. Pray to Obey

Hand each child a black footprint from the "Follow the Leader" activity.

Say: **Find a person with shoes the same color as the ones you're wearing. Decide who will go first. When I clap once, the first person will tell his or her partner one way he or she can follow God this week. When I clap two times, the other person will share. Exchange footprints as you talk with each other.**

Allow a few moments for children to exchange footprints. Be sure each child has a turn to talk with someone else. Then say: **Let's say a prayer asking God to help us follow and obey him more closely. Dear God, thank you for loving us and giving us directions to follow. Please help us follow you more closely each day, God. In Jesus' name, amen.**

Say: **As you leave today, take your footprints with you to remind you how important it is to obey God and to follow in his footsteps like Josiah.**

by Christine Yount

13. It's Good to Give to Others
(The Widow's Offering)

In Bible times, wealthy people were expected to visit God's Temple to pay Temple taxes and to give money to help the poor. But giving wasn't often in proportion to wealth. The story of the widow who gave all she had is a powerful example of selfless giving. The widow gave freely and cheerfully all she had to give.

Children are experts at selective giving. Joey finds it easy to give up a piece of candy when he has a whole bag, while Sarah freely gives away the doll she never plays with. It's much harder for children to give away something they want. Yet generous, cheerful giving is the kind of giving God desires. Use this lesson to help children realize that even the smallest gifts are of great value when they're given cheerfully and with love.

A POWERFUL POINT

Giving to others brings us joy.

A LOOK AT THE LESSON

1. Jelly Bean Pass (8 minutes)
2. A Bit of Background (8 minutes)
3. Sharing Sacks (9 minutes)
4. Offer to Give (8 minutes)
5. Food for Thought (7 minutes)
6. God Loves a Cheerful Giver (7 minutes)

A SPRINKLING OF SUPPLIES

Collect a Bible, a bag of colored jelly beans, small paper sacks, a roll of new pennies, glue, scissors, markers, construction paper, a paper plate, a box of graham crackers, and five photocopies of the "Money, Money!" handout (p. 68).

THE FUN-TO-LEARN LESSON

1. Jelly Bean Pass

(You'll need a Bible, a paper sack, and a bag of multicolored jelly beans. Before class, pour half the jelly beans into a paper sack.)

Have the children sit in a circle on the floor and hand each child three jelly beans. Do not hand out any green or red jelly beans. Tell children not to eat their candy yet.

Say: **We're going to play a giving game. I'll pass the bag of jelly beans to one of you. Without looking into the bag, choose a bean. If it's a color other than green or red, you may keep it. If you choose a red jelly bean, you must give a jelly bean to someone. If you choose a green jelly bean, you may ask another person to give you one of his or her beans.**

Play until everyone's had a turn to choose a jelly bean from the sack. Then

ask:

● **How did it feel to give away your jelly beans?**

● **Did anyone give away certain jelly beans? Why did you choose those particular beans?** (Some of the children will probably tell you they gave up their least favorite colors, the smallest beans, or funny-shaped beans.)

Say: **It's easy to give away things we don't like or want. But true giving means we're willing to offer everything we own to help someone else. Today we'll hear a Bible story about a woman who gave away all she had.**

Collect the "used" jelly beans and hand each child three fresh ones. Tell children they may now eat the jelly beans.

2. A Bit of Background

(You'll need a Bible and five photocopies of the "Money, Money!" handout on page 68. Use green paper for photocopying if possible. Cut out the money from the handouts before this activity.)

Sit on the floor and have the children sit in a circle around you. Open the Bible and say: **The Bible story today comes from the book of Mark** (12:41-44). **It's about a woman who gave all she had to help others. You can help me with the story.** Hand each child a handful of "money." Say: **Whenever I say the words "give," "given," or "gave," toss a few dollars in the air. If you run out of money, come sit in the center with me.**

Say: **One day, Jesus and his disciples were in Jerusalem. Jesus sat by the Temple offering box. This was where money was collected to pay Temple taxes and to help poor people. Jesus watched as people came to <u>give</u> their money. Jesus saw many rich people come to the offering box.**

The rich people wore fancy clothes and robes. Many of these people <u>gave</u> a lot of money.

Then Jesus saw a poor widow coming to the offering box. She didn't look like she had much to <u>give</u>. The poor widow <u>gave</u> two small coins. The coins she <u>gave</u> were only worth a few cents.

Jesus called his followers to him. He said, "This poor widow <u>gave</u> more than all those rich people. They <u>gave</u> only what they did not need. This woman is very poor, but she <u>gave</u> all she had; she <u>gave</u> all she had to live on."

Ask:

● **What was it like to give away your money?**

● **If you have money left, did you try to hold back giving your money? Why or why not?**

● **Was it easier to give when you had a lot? Explain.**

Say: **It's often easy to give freely when we have a lot of something. It's harder to give when we barely have enough for ourselves. The poor widow only had two small coins. That's all the money she had in the world.**

Ask:

● **Why do you think she gave everything she had?**

● **Which gift was better—the two coins or the riches the other people gave?**

Say: **Jesus teaches us that true giving doesn't depend on how much we give, but on the way we give. God wants us to give freely and with love. He wants us to give and share unselfishly.** Gather the play money and set it aside.

3. Sharing Sacks

(You'll need glue, scissors, construction paper scraps, markers, and a small paper sack for each child.)

Say: **There are many things to give and share with other people.**

Ask:

● **What are some things we can give or share with others?** (Answers may include food, toys, clothing, our talents, our help, our time, our ideas, and our love.)

Say: **Today we're going to decorate "sharing sacks" to remind us of ways to give freely to others. You may get into small groups and work together.**

Set out paper sacks, markers, glue, and construction paper scraps. Allow children time to decorate their sharing sacks. Suggest making paper handles and adding colorful paper streamers to the sides of the sacks. Circulate and affirm children as you notice them helping each other. Point out that God provides many ways we can give to others, and giving an encouraging word or help are two good ways.

When everyone's finished, let the kids display their creations. Say: **We'll be putting things in our sharing sacks to help us remember some of the things God wants us to give freely and lovingly.**

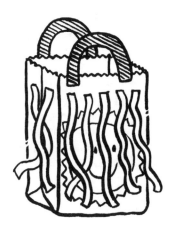

4. Offer to Give

(You'll need a paper plate, two pennies, and the play money from the handouts.)

Have children form a circle on the floor. Hold up the paper plate and say: **In church, we pass an offering plate. People put money in the offering plate just as the poor widow put her offering in the Temple box. Let's set the offering plate in the center of the circle and play a game. First you'll need something to give. I'll secretly give each of you some money. Don't let anyone see what you have to give or the game won't be as fun.**

Hand one child two pennies. Hand the rest of the children varying amounts of play money. Then say: **Some of you have play money to give, and one of you is like the poor widow who only has two small coins. We'll try to figure out who's the poor widow. I'll choose one of you to bring your offering to the offering plate. Before you put your offering in the plate, tell one thing you could give someone this week. Tell how much you have to give and set it in the offering plate. Then call on someone you think is the poor widow.**

Continue until everyone's had a turn to give an offering. Then ask:

● **Why do you think giving freely and with love is important?**

Say: **We know from the Bible story that money is one thing we can give. Now I'll give each of you a play dollar to put in your sharing sack, and then we'll look at another way God helps us give.**

5. Food for Thought

(You'll need a box of graham crackers and a paper plate.)

Before class set out three fewer graham cracker rectangles than there are children. (One graham cracker rectangle usually contains four smaller sections.)

Gather children together. Say: **God wants us to give freely and with love. When we give, we show God's love. I'd like to give you a snack.**

As you pass out the graham crackers, remind kids not to eat until everyone's been served. When you run out of crackers, say: **We don't have enough graham crackers for everybody.**

Ask:

● **Can you think of a way to help?**

Call on children to share their ideas. Point children to the idea of breaking the large crackers into smaller squares and sharing them. Let the children with crackers break them apart. Place the crackers on the paper plate and divide the graham crackers among the children.

When everyone's been served in equal amounts, say: **Before we enjoy our snack, let's pray. Dear God, thank you for giving us your love. Please help us look for ways we can give freely and with love. In Jesus' name, amen.**

As children enjoy their crackers, say: **You just showed me another way to give! When we freely share what we have, we're giving love. You also gave a good idea when you suggested breaking the crackers. There are many ways God helps us give.**

6. God Loves a Cheerful Giver

(You'll need a Bible and a roll of new pennies.)

Hold up the Bible and say: **The Bible teaches us how to give to others. Let's read what God's Word says.** Open the Bible to 2 Corinthians 9:7 and read it aloud. Then ask:

● **Why is it good to give cheerfully?**
● **Who can share about a time he**

or she felt happy giving something to someone?

Have children each find a partner. Then say: **Let's end our lesson by singing a fun song about cheerful giving. I'll give each set of partners nine pennies. Choose which partner will be the first penny holder. The other person will hold out his or her cupped hands. As we sing, the penny holder will drop one penny at a time into the cupped hands.**

Hand out the pennies. Then lead children in singing "God Loves a Cheerful Giver" to the tune of "Ten Little Indians." As you sing each offering, kids should drop one penny at a time into their partners' cupped hands. Sing the second verse without dropping pennies. Then switch penny holders and repeat the song to give each partner a chance to drop pennies.

"GOD LOVES A CHEERFUL GIVER"

One little, two little, three little offerings,
four little, five little, six little offerings,
seven little, eight little, nine little offerings—
God loves a cheerful giver!
I will help and give my time.
I'll be glad to share what's mine.
I will let my giving shine.
God loves a cheerful giver!

(Repeat for the second partner.)

When you're done singing, distribute the sharing sacks and hand each child a shiny penny to drop inside. Then say: **As you leave today, take this penny to remind you that giving freely and with love makes us shine with happiness.**

by Ellen Javernick

MONEY, MONEY!

Directions: Photocopy this handout on green paper. Cut out the dollar bills.

14. Time With God (Mary and Martha)

The story of Mary and Martha, found in the book of Luke, reminds us how we're often buried in the "busyness" of our daily lives. Responsibilities and commitments grab top priority. If we're not careful, we lose sight of the simple beauty and importance of quiet time with God. Mary and Martha help us see the importance of being still before God. And busy or not, God loves it when we spend time with him.

Use this lesson to help children realize the importance of spending time with God.

A POWERFUL POINT

God wants us to spend quiet time with him.

A LOOK AT THE LESSON

1. Broom-Zoom Relay (7 minutes)
2. Silent Scripture (8 minutes)
3. Martha and Mary Mimes (9 minutes)
4. Sweet-Time Snacks (8 minutes)
5. Do Not Disturb (9 minutes)
6. Spending Time With God (6 minutes)

A SPRINKLING OF SUPPLIES

Collect a Bible, newspapers, masking tape, a wastebasket, a scarf, a few plastic knives, napkins, peanut butter, honey, and crackers. You'll also need to gather stickers, scissors, ribbon, crayons, regular paper, construction paper, markers, and one photocopy of the "Do Not Disturb" handout (p. 73) for each child.

THE FUN-TO-LEARN LESSON

1. Broom-Zoom Relay

(You'll need newspapers, masking tape, and a wastebasket. Before this activity, make two newspaper brooms. For each broom, twist three sheets of newspapers together tightly at one end. Wrap the twisted end with masking tape to make a sturdy handle. Leave the other end twisted loosely to sweep.)

Set the wastebasket at one end of the room. Have children form two groups and stand at the opposite end of the room. Give each group a paper broom, then give each child a half sheet of newspaper to crumple into a wad. Then say: **We're going to have a race called Broom Zoom. The first person in each line will set his or her paper wad on the floor. You'll sweep the paper wads to the wastebasket with these paper brooms and toss the paper wads away. Then hop back to your group and hand the broom to the next person. We'll see how quickly you can get the paper wads in the wastebasket.**

After the race, set the paper brooms aside. Gather the kids into a group on the floor. Say: **You looked busy with all that sweeping and cleaning!**

69

Ask:

● **Who can tell about another time he or she was busy doing something?**

● **Were you ever so busy that you didn't have time to pray or read the Bible? Explain.**

Say: **It's good to have things to do, but sometimes we get too busy. We forget to spend time with God. Isn't it nice that God loves us no matter how busy we are? Today we'll hear a story about two sisters. One sister was so busy, she nearly forgot to listen to Jesus.**

2. Silent Scripture

(You'll need a Bible, crayons, and paper.)

Seat children around you on the floor and say: **Being busy is nice, but spending quiet time with God is nice, too, and very important. Let's read what the Bible says about being still and quiet with God.** Open the Bible to Psalm 46:10a and read it aloud. Then ask:

● **What are some ways we can spend quiet time with God?** (Lead children to think of answers such as reading the Bible, praying, going to church, and helping other people.)

Say: **Let's play a quiet game and spend time with God's Word. We'll form three groups, and I'll give each group a few crayons and a sheet of paper. When I whisper "go," each group can work together to draw a picture of someone spending quiet time with God. Be sure each person has a turn to help draw or color the picture. There's one rule: No talking allowed! When your picture is finished, silently join hands in your group.**

When you notice that each group has finished and joined hands, softly say: **In this quiet moment, let's pray together. Dear God, we thank you for giving us many ways to keep busy. We thank you for giving us time to be quiet and still with you. Help us know how much you love us no matter what we're doing. Amen.**

Let groups each tell about the pictures they made.

Say: **Each of you was busy even while you were quiet with God. Now let's quietly read a Scripture verse.** Read Psalm 46:10a aloud or call on a volunteer to read the verse for the class. Then say: **I'd like to tell you a Bible story about two sisters. One sister was busy with dust and dishes; the other sister was busy listening to Jesus.**

3. Martha and Mary Mimes

(You'll need a Bible and a scarf.)

Hold up the Bible. Point to it and say: **The Bible story today comes from the book of Luke. It's about two of Jesus' friends. Their names are Mary** (put the scarf over your head) **and Martha** (place the scarf around your shoulders). **You can help me tell this story. When I say "Martha" and put the scarf around my shoulders, jump up and pretend to clean house. You could sweep or dust or mop floors. When I say "Mary" and put the scarf on my head, silently drop to your knees and fold your hands like you're praying.** Practice the story actions a few times. When your kids feel comfortable, begin the Bible story.

Jesus had two friends who were sisters. One of the sisters was named <u>Martha</u>, and the other sister was named <u>Mary</u>. One day, Jesus came to visit them. <u>Martha</u> was worried the house wasn't clean enough. So <u>Martha</u> scrubbed and dusted and

mopped and cleaned and worked very hard to make the house nice. "Where is <u>Mary</u>?" she thought. "Must I do all the work alone? Must I fix all the food by myself?" <u>Martha</u> went to find her sister, <u>Mary</u>. And guess where she found her!

<u>Mary</u> was sitting at Jesus' feet! <u>Mary</u> was listening to Jesus teach about God. <u>Martha</u> couldn't believe it. Here she was, being so busy, and her sister, <u>Mary</u>, was *sitting* with Jesus!

<u>Martha</u> looked at Jesus and said, "Don't you care that my sister left me to do *all* the work?"

Jesus said, "<u>Martha</u>, don't worry about so many things. You're filling your time being busy, but your sister knows only *one* thing is important. <u>Mary</u> chose the better way."

Set aside the scarf and gather children into a circle on the floor. Ask:

● **Why do you think Jesus said Mary chose the better way?**

● **Which do you think was more important: cleaning the house or listening to Jesus? Why?**

Say: **God loves us no matter what keeps us busy or how hard we work. God wants us to have time for many things, including work and play. But it's also important to find time every day to spend with God. We don't want to be like Martha and get so busy that we forget to spend quiet time with God.**

4. Sweet-Time Snacks

(You'll need peanut butter, honey, crackers, napkins, and a few plastic knives.)

Create some exciting fun by having your kids prepare snacks in an assembly line. Assign jobs for the children in the following order: cracker passers,

peanut butter spreaders (who spread peanut butter on the crackers), and honey helpers (who add honey to the crackers).

When enough crackers have been made for each child to have two, have the children clean up their work area and wipe their sticky hands. Then gather the kids around a table. Hand each child a napkin, a plain cracker, and a peanut butter-and-honey cracker. Say: **Let's see which cracker takes you longer to eat: the plain one or the peanut butter-and-honey cracker.** Allow time for the children to eat both crackers. Then ask:

● **Which cracker did you spend more time eating? Why?**

Say: **Spending time with God is a lot like eating the cracker with peanut butter and honey. It's sweet, and it takes a while to get the whole flavor. When we spend time with God and don't rush, it's a real treat!**

Let the kids enjoy the remaining peanut butter-and-honey crackers.

5. Do Not Disturb

(You'll need construction paper, scissors, glue, ribbons, stickers, markers, and a photocopy of the "Do Not Disturb" handout on page 73 for each child.)

Have the children sit at a table. Ask:

● **When do people use Do Not Disturb signs?**

● **How can a Do Not Disturb sign help us spend time with God?**

● **When are some "do not disturb" times can you spend with God?** (Answers may include "When I'm reading the Bible," "When I'm praying," or "When I'm listening to God and thinking about his Word.")

Say: **Let's make Do Not Disturb doorknob hangers to use when we**

spend quiet times with God.

Give each child a photocopy of the "Do Not Disturb" handout. Have kids color and cut out the doorknob hangers. Tell children to carefully cut out the inside circle from the hanger. Then have them decorate their hangers with ribbons and stickers. As the children work, read the verse on the doorknob hanger aloud.

When everyone is finished, say: **Get with two other kids. Show them your decorated hanger as you tell one way you can be still with God this week.**

Allow a minute for the children to share in their small groups. Then say: **God loves us whether we're busy or not. And spending time with God is a good way to tell God you love *him*.**

6. Spending Time With God

(Use American Sign Language or your own symbols to share this message of God's love and your love with the kids.)

With kids seated around you on the floor, ask:

● **Mary sat quietly at Jesus' feet. How was that a way of saying she loved him?**

● **What do you think I'm saying?** Do the following motions: point to yourself, cross your arms over your chest, then point to the children. Call on kids to tell what they think you silently said ("I love you"). Have the children turn to the two people sitting beside them and in sign language say, "God loves you" (point upward, cross your arms over your chest, and point at the other person).

Say: **Let's sing an action song about spending time with God. We'll sing the words out loud with the motions the first time. Then we'll repeat the song while we whisper the words with the motions.**

Lead the children in singing "Yes, God, I Love You" to the tune of "Jesus Loves Me."

"YES, GOD, I LOVE YOU"

When I'm busy as a bee,
(fly around the room)
I miss the things God's telling me.
(Cover ears or eyes.)
If I'm running here and there,
(jog in place)
I forget to say I care.

Yes, God, I love you.
(Nod yes, point to yourself, cross arms over your chest, and point upward.)
Yes, God, I love you.
(Nod yes, point to yourself, cross arms over your chest, and point upward.)
Yes, God, I love you.
(Nod yes, point to yourself, cross arms over your chest, and point upward.)
I'll spend my time with you.
(Point to yourself, hold your hands palms up, and point upward.)

Say: **As you leave today, remember to spend some time being quiet with God. And spend time saying thank you to God for how he loves you— just the way you are!**

by Debbie Trafton O'Neal

DO NOT DISTURB

Directions: Color the doorknob hanger. Cut out the hanger and the center circle. Put it on your doorknob to let people know you're spending quiet time with God!

15. We're Forgiven (The Woman Who Wept)

While young children may not fully understand the concept of sin, they're developing a solid sense of right and wrong. They're also learning that the world assigns right and wrong differently than God does. The story of the woman who wept at Jesus' feet is a good example of God's forgiveness. The woman came to Jesus with love and the desire to turn away from the wrong things she'd done—and Jesus forgave her.

Use this lesson to help children learn that no matter what they've done, God loves them and offers his forgiveness.

A POWERFUL POINT

God forgives us when we do something wrong.

A LOOK AT THE LESSON

1. Messy Marks (9 minutes)
2. At the Feet of Jesus (9 minutes)
3. Do the Two-Step (8 minutes)
4. A Lot of Scents! (9 minutes)
5. Now You See It, Now You Don't (8 minutes)
6. God's Forgiving Heart (5 minutes)

A SPRINKLING OF SUPPLIES

Gather a Bible; two or three red watercolor markers; a piece of white, cotton cloth; a bucket; water; bleach; and liquid detergent. You'll also need to collect perfume, grapes, paper plates, red and green crayons, three oranges, a bag of dried cloves, paper towels, and a knife.

THE FUN-TO-LEARN LESSON

1. Messy Marks

(You'll need two or three red watercolor markers; a piece of white, cotton cloth; a bucket; water; bleach; and liquid detergent. Before this activity, fill a small bucket half full of water. Add a cup of bleach and 2 tablespoons of detergent to the water. Set the bucket aside and out of reach of the children until later.)

Have kids stand in a line at one end of the room. Lay the piece of cloth at the other end of the room, opposite the children. Set the red watercolor markers beside the fabric.

Say: **Let's number off by threes.** Help children count off in line by threes. **When I call out your number, hop to the white cloth at the other end of the room. Choose a marker and draw a line or some kind of mark on the cloth. Then hop back, and I'll call out another number.**

More than one child will be hopping and drawing at one time. Continue until everyone has had a turn. Then have the kids sit at a table. Set the bucket with the bleach and detergent in the center of the table on newspapers or paper towels. Hold up the cloth with the red marks. Ask:

● **How did you feel about making marks on the white cloth?**

● **Does it look better clean or marked up? Explain.**

Say: **The marks on this cloth make it look unclean and messy. The marks are like things we do wrong. When we do things that God tells us are wrong, it's like making marks on our hearts.**

Ask:

● **What are some things God tells us are wrong?** (Answers may include lying, cheating, stealing, being mean to others, disobeying God, killing, and swearing.)

● **How do you feel if you do one of those wrong things?**

Say: **We've all done things that God tells us are wrong. These are called sins. Doing things God says are wrong is like making marks on our hearts. We become dirty inside. We want to find a way to become clean and fresh again. We want our marks to be taken away.**

Dip the cloth into the bucket. Be careful to keep dry the portion you're holding. Help the children each take a turn slowly dipping the cloth in the water. Be careful not to let any of the bleach water get on clothes or hands. Say: **Jesus is the only one who can make us clean by forgiving the wrong things we've done. Today we'll hear about a woman who did things God said were wrong. We'll learn how Jesus forgave those wrong things— which we call sins—and how the woman could be God's friend.**

Let the cloth soak in the bleach water until later. Set the bucket out of reach of the children.

2. At the Feet of Jesus

(You'll need a Bible, grapes, and perfume.)

Ask:

● **What's something you've done wrong?**

● **How did you feel when you knew it was wrong but you did it anyway?**

● **What it was like when someone forgave you?**

Open your Bible to Luke 7:36-50. Hold up the Bible and say: **The Bible story today is found in the book of Luke. It's about a woman who felt awful about the wrong things she'd done. We'll act out the story, and I'll lead you in the actions.**

Jesus had been invited to eat dinner with a group of men called the Pharisees. The Pharisees thought they were very good and knew all about God. (Make prayer hands and turn your eyes to heaven, looking snooty.) **The Pharisees liked to tell other people what they were doing wrong.** (Waggle your first finger at someone else.)

As Jesus ate dinner with the Pharisees (hand each child a grape to eat)**, a woman came into the room. She didn't say a word, but she walked over to Jesus.** (Walk forward a few steps.) **She kneeled at Jesus' feet.** (Kneel with your head hung low.) **The woman felt very sad because she knew she'd done things that were wrong. She began to cry softly.** (Make soft crying sounds and sniffles.) **The woman's tears fell on Jesus' feet, and she wiped his feet with her hair.** (Lean your hair to the floor.) **Then she took a bottle of perfume from her pocket. She poured the precious perfume on Jesus' feet.** (Carry the perfume bottle to each child. Allow them to put a dab on their fingertips and then dab it on their feet.) **The Pharisees, who thought they couldn't do anything wrong** (prayer hands and eyes to heaven, looking snooty), **told Jesus the woman was bad because she'd done many wrong things.** (Waggle your first finger at someone else.) **Jesus looked with love at the woman who was softly crying.** (Make soft crying sounds and sniffles.) **Jesus saw she was sorry for what she'd done. He saw there was love in her heart.** (Cross your hands over your heart.) **Jesus said, "Because of your great love and faith, you're forgiven for the wrong things you've done." The woman looked up and smiled at Jesus with great love!** (Smile and cross your hands over your heart.) **She felt clean and new already and wouldn't do those wrong things again.**

Ask:

● **Why do you think Jesus forgave the woman?**

● **How do you think she felt when Jesus forgave everything she'd done wrong?**

● **Why do you think the woman didn't do those same wrong things anymore?**

Say: **Jesus loves us so much. He knows we've done things God says are wrong, and yet he loves us anyway. And just as Jesus forgave the woman in this story, Jesus will forgive us.**

3. Do the Two-Step

(You'll need paper plates and red and green crayons. Before this activity, color one side of a paper plate red and the other side green. Count out enough paper plates for each child to have one.)

Ask:

● **Why is it important that we be forgiven by God?**

Say: **In the Bible story, a woman came to Jesus with perfume to pour on his feet. She came with tears of sadness for the wrong things she'd done. She wanted Jesus to forgive her. Then she stopped doing those wrong things. Let's play a game to find out the two steps we can take to be forgiven.**

Hand each child a paper plate. Have them stand side by side at one end of the room, facing you. You will stand at the opposite end with the red-and-green paper plate.

Say: **I'll hold up this red-and-green plate. When you see green, walk slowly toward me. When you see red, stop and set your plate on the floor. Then do the "two-step": first stand on your plate on one foot and say, "Jesus, please forgive me." Then twirl on your plate and say, "I'll turn away from wrong." Let's try it.** Hold up the red plate a few times and have the children practice stepping and twirling on their plates. When they seem comfortable with the words and the steps, hold up the green side of your plate to begin.

When all the children have reached you, gather them in a circle on the floor. Ask:

● **What are the two steps we can take to be forgiven like the woman in the story?** (Lead children to say, "Asking Jesus' forgiveness" and "Not doing the same wrong things again.")

Say: **Jesus doesn't want us to do things God says are wrong. Because Jesus loves us, he wants to forgive us. Let's make a sweet-smelling gift to remind us how sweet Jesus' love is.**

4. A Lot of Scents!

(You'll need a bag of dried cloves, three oranges, and paper towels.

Before this activity, you'll need to carefully peel the oranges so you'll have whole quarter sections of the peel. To do this, simply make two shallow, vertical cuts around the orange from the top back to the top. Gently begin at the top of the orange and loosen one quarter section of the orange peel at a time.)

Set the orange peels and the orange sections on paper towels on a table. Put the cloves next to the orange peels. Group the kids around the table. Ask:

● **What did the woman in the story do to Jesus' feet?** (Answers may include that she cried on his feet, she wiped them with her hair, and she poured perfume on them.

Say: **In Jesus' day, perfume was very special and cost a lot of money. Whenever it was poured on someone, it was a sign of great love and honor.** Hold up the oranges and the peels. **Perfume was made from the juices and oils of different fruits, like these oranges. We're going to make sweet-smelling oranges to share with people we love, just like the woman in the story shared her sweet perfume with Jesus.**

Hand each child a paper towel and a section of orange peel. Show the children how to press the pointed end of a clove into the outside of the orange peel. Press three or four cloves into each peel. As they work, point out to children that the woman's perfume offering was her way of asking Jesus to forgive her. It was a way for her to tell Jesus she loved him and wanted to follow him.

When the children are finished, say: **Close your eyes and smell your orange peels.**

Ask:

● **How do they smell?**

Set the "perfumed" peels aside to take home at the end of the lesson. Divide the oranges for the kids to share. Say: **Let's say a prayer thanking Jesus for his forgiveness. Dear God, thank you for promising to forgive the wrong things we do. We ask Jesus for your forgiveness, and we want to follow Jesus. Please help us to not do the same wrong things anymore. In Jesus' name, amen.**

5. Now You See It, Now You Don't

(You'll need a Bible.)

Gather the children around the table. Say: **When we've done something God says is wrong, and we're truly sorry, we can ask him to forgive us. And he will.**

Hold up the Bible and say: **Let's see what the Bible says about God's forgiveness.**

Open the Bible to 1 John 9 and read it aloud. Then say: **When we tell God we're sorry for the wrong things we've done, he'll forgive us. Let's see if the cloth we marked up is clean.** Set the bucket containing the bleach and water on the table. Gently pull out the cloth and wring out the excess water. Hold up the cloth. The cloth may be bleached clean or a few of the marks may still be seen slightly. Ask:

● **What happened to the marks?**

● **Do you think any eraser or any person can make the wrong things we've done disappear? Why or why not?**

● **Who's the only one who can forgive the wrong things we do?**

If all of the marks haven't been removed, say: **Because there were so many marks, the cloth wasn't made absolutely perfect—but it's much cleaner and brighter than before.**

When we're forgiven for the wrong things we do, we're much cleaner, but we still aren't perfect. That's why we need Jesus in our lives every day! When our hearts feel fresh and new and clean, we're able to be God's friends again.

6. God's Forgiving Heart

Cup your hands and say: **The woman in the Bible story asked for forgiveness. She knew she'd done wrong things and wanted to feel clean and good again. The woman came to Jesus because she knew he could help her heart feel better. I'm holding a pretend heart. I'll pass my heart to the person beside me and** say, "**I love Jesus and want God to forgive me.**" **Then it's that person's turn to pass on the heart.**

When each person has had a turn to pass the heart, say: **God wants us to be happy and forgiven, just like the woman in the Bible story. When we ask God to forgive us, he'll forgive us.**

Hand out the scented orange peels the children made earlier and say: **Remember to give your sweet-smelling orange to someone you love. You can tell that person how much God loves him or her and how he forgives the wrong things we've done.**

by Vicki Shannon

16. Everyone's Welcome (Roman Centurion)

In the town of Capernaum lay a dying servant. Close by stood the Roman army officer who was his master. Though the Roman centurion was greatly disliked by Hebrew people, he asked Jesus' help in healing the ailing servant. Jesus could have refused, for the Roman soldier was born in a different country and lived in a culture that did not love God. But instead of differences, Jesus saw the man's love and faith. Jesus accepted the Roman centurion and healed his servant.

Differences among people often make children feel uncomfortable. Anything from physical differences to clothing styles to manners of speech can keep children from getting to know the new child in class or church. Children need to learn that people are different because God made us different. And God wants us to accept and love each person regardless of differences. Use this lesson to encourage children to accept and love others as God does.

A POWERFUL POINT

Accept and love all people as God does.

A LOOK AT THE LESSON

1. Around the World (8 minutes)
2. Centurion Shields (9 minutes)
3. Faraway Flying Disks (8 minutes)
4. Spread Your Love Around the World (9 minutes)
5. Love Knots (8 minutes)
6. God Loves Us All! (5 minutes)

A SPRINKLING OF SUPPLIES

Gather a Bible, newsprint, a roll of aluminum foil, a stapler, paper plates, cardboard or poster board, scissors, paper, jam, two plastic knives, napkins, a rice cake for each child, yarn, and a hole punch.

THE FUN-TO-LEARN LESSON

1. Around the World

(You'll need newsprint.)

Crumple two sheets of newsprint to use as paper balls. Have the children stand in a circle. Hold one of the paper balls and say: **Let's pretend we're standing in a circle that goes all the way around the world. I'll toss this ball to someone on the other side of the world, and they'll toss the ball to someone else. We'll continue until the ball has traveled to each person around the world and ends up back with me.**

When the ball has made it to each person and back to you, repeat the game using two paper balls. Then have the children sit down where they're standing. Ask:

● **If we'd forgotten someone, would the paper balls have traveled all around the circle? Explain.**

Say: **Each person in our circle is important. You helped the ball go farther, and that's how the ball made it around the world. God loves us, and each of us is important to him. Even though we may look different, speak in different languages, or enjoy different foods, God accepts and loves us. That's how God's love spreads around the world. God wants us to accept and love all people, too.**

2. Centurion Shields

(You'll need a Bible, a roll of aluminum foil, a stapler, cardboard or poster board, scissors, and one paper plate for each child. Before this activity, cut cardboard or poster board into strips that are 1 inch wide and 6 inches long.)

Hold up the Bible and say: **The Bible story today is about a man who was a Roman centurion. Roman centurions were officers who were in charge of about 100 Roman soldiers. But most Romans didn't love God. Before I share the story of the Roman centurion, we're going to make shields like the soldiers carried. The shields will help us tell the Bible story.**

Have children sit in a circle. Hand each child a paper plate. Set the roll of aluminum foil, the stapler, and the strips of cardboard in the center of the circle. Show them how to wrap their paper plates with aluminum foil. Then staple a cardboard strip to the back of the plate to create a handle for carrying the shield. As the children work, ask questions such as "Do you think God loved the Romans even though they didn't love God? Why?" and "Why does God accept all people?"

When everyone's finished, open the Bible to Luke 7:1-10. Say: **The Bible story today is found in the book of Luke. You can use your shields to help tell the story. Each time I say, "Roman centurion," leap to your feet, hold up your shield, and shout, "God accepts me!" Then quietly sit down and listen for the next time I say, "Roman centurion."**

In a town called Capernaum, there lived a man who was a <u>Roman</u> <u>centurion</u>. He was a brave soldier and an important man. But the Romans were people who didn't know or love God.

The <u>Roman</u> <u>centurion</u> had a servant who was sick and about to die. He felt sad and wanted to help his servant.

The <u>Roman</u> <u>centurion</u> had heard about Jesus and how he had healed people. So when Jesus came to town to teach people about God, the <u>Roman centurion</u> sent a group of Jewish men to talk with Jesus.

He told the men to ask Jesus to come and make his servant well. The men said, "Please come because this officer is worthy of your help! He loves our people, and he even built a temple for us to worship God."

Jesus was touched by the <u>Roman centurion's</u> faith. After all, the Roman people didn't know or love God! Yet the <u>Roman</u> <u>centurion</u> knew Jesus could make his servant well again.

As Jesus neared the officer's house, the <u>Roman</u> <u>centurion</u> again sent men to talk to Jesus. "The officer says he isn't worthy to have you come into his house. The <u>Roman</u> <u>centurion</u> knows that if you just say the words from here, his servant will be healed!"

When Jesus heard this, he turned to the crowd of people who were following him. Jesus said, "This is the greatest faith I have found any-

where—even among God's people!" And Jesus healed the <u>Roman</u> <u>centurion's</u> servant.

Have the kids sit on their shields in a circle on the floor. Ask:

● **Why do you think the Roman centurion believed Jesus could heal his servant?**

● **Did Jesus love the Roman soldier even though he was from a different country? How do you know?**

● **Why did Jesus say the centurion had the greatest faith he'd ever seen?**

Say: **God loves all people. He accepts all people and loves and cares for them. God wants us to accept and love all people, too. When we accept others, we're showing God's love to the world.**

3. Faraway Flying Disks

(You'll need three sheets of paper and the shields from the previous activity. Before this activity, write each of these words on a separate sheet of paper: "state," "city," and "country.")

Have the children line up at one end of the room, then scatter the three papers at the opposite end of the room. Say: **Let's play a game to help us learn some of the different places people live. Knowing about the places people live helps us accept them and share God's love.**

We'll use the shields we made as flying disks. When I say "go," we'll toss our disks toward the papers. Then we'll take turns telling the name of a city, a state, or a country— whichever your disk lands closest to. If you need help with the name of a place, we'll pitch in to help. After you tell the name of a place, we'll shout, "God loves the people in (that state, city, or country)!"

Help small children name locations by asking where their grandparents or other relatives and friends live.

When everyone's had a turn, say: **There are so many people in different places of the world. Isn't it nice that God accepts and loves every one of us?**

4. Spread Your Love Around the World

(You'll need jam, two plastic knives, napkins, and a rice cake for each child.)

Say: **The Roman centurion was accepted and loved by God even though he was from a part of the world where most people didn't know God. Let's make a snack from another part of God's world.**

Hold up a rice cake and say: **Many people in countries such as China and Japan enjoy eating rice cakes. Since rice cakes are round, let's pretend they're the world. We've been learning that God spreads his love all around the world because he accepts everyone. God's love is sweet, so we'll pretend this jam is his love. See if you can spread God's love around the world!**

Hand children each a rice cake and let them spread jam on it. As children are making their snacks, ask questions such as "Why do you think God wants us to accept others?" or "What might happen if everyone in the world accepted and loved each other?"

When everyone has finished, say: **Before we eat our snacks, let's say a prayer thanking God for helping us love and accept all people. Dear God, thank you for loving us the way we are. Please help us love and accept all people. Help us know we're all your children. Amen.** Let kids eat their rice cakes.

5. Love Knots

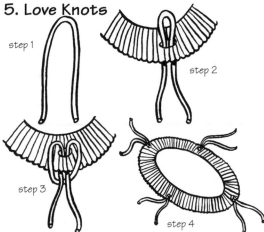

step 1

step 2

step 3

step 4

(You'll need yarn, scissors, and a hole punch. Before this activity, cut four 12-inch lengths of yarn for each child.)

Have each child find a friend or two to work with. Say: **We've been learning that God accepts and loves all people and that God wants us to accept others, too.**

Ask:

● **What are some ways we can show others we love and accept them?**

Say: **If we accepted everyone as God does, then the whole world would be filled with love! We'll make "love knots" to remind us that God wants us to accept and love people just as he does.**

Have children punch four holes around the edges of their paper-plate shields. Tell the children not to punch the holes too close to the edge. Let each child choose four pieces of yarn. Show the kids how to fold the length of yarn in half and poke the looped end through one of the holes. Pull the yarn halfway through. Thread the loose ends through the looped end. Then pull the ends taut. This makes a love knot. Continue making three more love knots. Encourage partners to help each other.

When everyone's finished, have part-ners join with one other pair or trio. Have them sit together, holding their decorated shields. Say: **Decide who will go first in your group. Then that person will touch one of his or her love knots and tell the name of a person he or she loves and accepts. Then the next person touches one of his or her knots and says a name, and so on. Continue around your group until each person has touched all four of his or her love knots.**

6. God Loves Us All!

Gather the children into one group. Say: **Let's end our time together by learning a new action rhyme that helps us remember that God always loves us and accepts us. Shake your shield as we say, "God will always love us."**

Lead the children in the following action rhyme:

Up, down, all around,
(up on tiptoes, squat down, and turn around)
God accepts and loves you!
(Touch someone with your shield.)
Out, in, touch my chin;
(lean forward, lean backward, and touch your chin.)
God accepts and loves you!
(Touch someone with your shield.)
Left, right, day and night,
(hop left, hop right, hop left, hop right)
God accepts and loves you!
(Touch someone with your shield.)
God accepts and loves you—and I will, too!
(Wave your shield in a circle.)

Say: **God wants us to love and accept all people, just as he does. Show your family your love knots as you tell them about the Roman centurion who was loved and accepted.**

by Nanette Goings

17. You're A-OK (Cornelius and Peter)

Peter was unsure about Cornelius because Cornelius was a Gentile and ate strange foods. In focusing on Cornelius' differences, Peter nearly missed the most important thing both men had in common—their desire to serve Jesus. When Peter finally understood that God wants us to appreciate one another, Peter accepted Cornelius and taught him about Jesus!

Children are thrown together in open classrooms with teachers and peers. It's important for them to learn to appreciate the gifts others have to offer. Use this lesson to help children learn to appreciate others and to realize we're all special to God.

A POWERFUL POINT

It's important to appreciate the people around us.

A LOOK AT THE LESSON

1. Paint Pot (8 minutes)
2. You Choose (8 minutes)
3. Peter and Cornelius (9 minutes)
4. Give and Take (7 minutes)
5. I Appreciate You (9 minutes)
6. Many Yet One (9 minutes)

A SPRINKLING OF SUPPLIES

Gather a Bible, paper, cellophane tape, markers, pencils, a bedsheet, a few stuffed animals, small sacks, a bag of wrapped candies, and poster board.

THE FUN-TO-LEARN LESSON

1. Paint Pot

Have the children line up at one end of the room. Clear the area in the center of the room so the children will have room to move freely. Designate one corner of the room as the "paint pot."

Say: **We're going to begin our time together with a game called Paint Pot. I'll choose someone to be the Painter. The Painter will call out the name of any color. If you're wearing that color, you must run to the other side of the room and touch the wall without being tagged by the Painter. If you're tagged, go to the paint pot and wait until all the colors have been caught.**

After the Painter has called a few colors, choose a child from the paint pot to be the new Painter. Play until all the children have been tagged. Then have the kids sit in a circle on the floor. Say: **It's fun to wear different colors. Each color is different, yet every color is nice.**

Ask:

● **Who can tell us his or her favorite color?**

● **Why do you think God created so many colors?**

Say: **We appreciate every color because God made each one. Some of us are wearing the same colors and some are wearing different ones. But each color looks nice! Just as we ap-**

preciate all sorts of different colors, God wants us to appreciate all people. Today we'll hear a Bible story about a man who learned to appreciate someone who seemed different.

2. You Choose

(You'll need paper, cellophane tape, and a marker. Before this activity, write the letter A on one sheet of paper and the letter B on another. Tape the papers to opposite corners of the room.)

Say: **God made each of us to be special. There are some things about us that are alike and some things that are very different. Let's play a game to help us learn some of the ways we're alike and different. I'll ask a question and give two choices as answers. Choose the answer** *you* **like best and run to that corner of the room. Let's try one for practice:**

● **If you're playing a game, which would you rather play: A, basketball; or B, dominoes? If you choose A for basketball, run to the A paper. If you choose B for dominoes, run to the B paper.** As soon as the children are comfortable with how to play the game, continue with the following questions and choices.

● **Which would you choose for dessert: A, chocolate cake; or B, cherry pie?**

● **Which would you choose to be when you grow up: A, a teacher; or B, a sports star?**

● **If you were a person in the Bible, would you choose to be: A, Noah; or B, Ruth?**

● **Which would you choose for a birthday gift: A, a new bike; or B, a trip to the amusement park?**

● **Where would you choose to go on vacation: A, the mountains; or B, the ocean?**

After the game, sit in a circle on the floor. Say: **Isn't it nice that we're alike and different in so many ways? God made each of us special, and we can appreciate the special ways we're alike and different. Today, we'll learn about a man named Cornelius, who was different from Peter. But God wanted Peter to appreciate Cornelius and be glad he was different.**

3. Peter and Cornelius

(You'll need a Bible, a bedsheet, and a few stuffed animals.)

Have children sit on the floor in a circle. Open your Bible to Acts 10 and 11. Hold up the Bible and say: **The Bible story today is from the book of Acts. It's about a man who was different from Peter. The man's name was Cornelius. Cornelius wasn't a Jew like Peter, and many Jews thought they were the only ones God loved.**

Ask:

● **What might it be like if God loved only one person?**

Continue: **Peter thought God didn't love Cornelius. And Peter knew that Cornelius ate different foods than he ate. Cornelius ate different kinds of meat that Peter thought weren't good to eat. Peter was afraid to be friends with Cornelius. In fact, Peter wasn't even sure he should** *talk* **with Cornelius or tell him about Jesus.**

Ask:

● **Do you think it was fair of Peter to avoid Cornelius this way? Why or why not?**

● **What would you do if someone you knew wanted to learn about Jesus?**

Bring out the bedsheet. Say: **Cornelius really wanted Peter to tell him about Jesus. But Peter ignored him. Then one night, Peter had a strange dream. He dreamed of a large sheet**

in the sky. Have the children stand up. Spread the sheet out in the center of the circle and let each child hold the sheet around the edge. Then say: **Peter dreamed that all sorts of different animals were in the sheet.** Toss one stuffed animal at a time into the sheet. As you toss each one in, call out what kind of animal it is.

Then ask:

● **Wasn't that a strange dream? What do you think God was telling Peter in that dream?**

Say: **God wanted Peter to know it was fine to eat any foods. God wanted Peter to know that Cornelius wasn't bad because he ate different foods. God was telling Peter to be friends with Cornelius and to tell Cornelius about Jesus!**

Ask:

● **Why do you think God wanted Peter to tell Cornelius about Jesus?**

Say: **God made us special, and he wants us to appreciate each other's differences. We're all special, we're all different, and we're God's children. Let's play a fun game about Peter and his strange dream from God. As we say a rhyme, we'll toss the stuffed animals high into the air and catch them on the sheet.**

Repeat the following rhyme. On the counts of one and two, lightly bounce the stuffed animals by tightening and loosening the sheet. Then toss the animals up in the air on the count of three. When you reach the end of the rhyme, toss the animals up with each word of "all about Jesus!"

One, two, three, (toss) **Peter had to see,**

Three, two, one, (toss) **that God loves everyone.**

Four, five, six, seven, (toss) **the animals fell from heaven.**

Eight comes next, then nine, (toss) **God made the dream a sign.**

Ten, eleven, twelve, (toss) **then Peter'd want to tell...**

all about Jesus!

Repeat the rhyme two or three times, then set the sheet and stuffed animals aside. Say: **God wants us to accept and appreciate all people as he does. Each person is special, and we can be happy about those special things. Just as Peter listened to God and accepted Cornelius, we can accept and appreciate other people, too.**

4. Give and Take

(You'll need one stuffed animal.)

Have children sit in a circle on the floor. Ask:

● **How would you feel if you wanted to learn about Jesus but no one would tell you?**

Say: **Let's play a game all about giving and taking.**

Choose a child to be the center person. Form two groups with the rest of the class. Say: **This group will be the Givers and will try to give the center person this stuffed animal. This group will be the Takers and will try to keep the stuffed animal away from the center person. There's one rule— the Takers must hold hands and not let go. Let's have the Takers stand in a circle around the center person. The Givers can surround the Takers.**

Hand the stuffed animal to someone on the Givers team. Have them work to get the toy to the person in the center. Encourage the Givers to try passing, rolling, or tossing the toy. If the Takers get the toy, switch groups and choose a new center person.

When each group has been both Takers and Givers, ask:

● **What was it like trying to give**

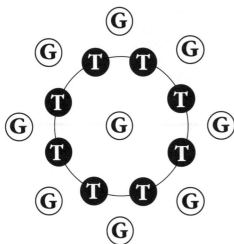

the toy to the center person?

● **How was the person in the center like Cornelius?**

● **Who didn't want Cornelius to learn about Jesus?**

Say: **Just as the center person wanted to get the stuffed animal, Cornelius wanted to get information about Jesus. God wanted Peter to appreciate Cornelius and his differences. Even though there are many differences in us, there are lots of things we can appreciate in one another.**

5. I Appreciate You

(You'll need small sacks, markers, and a bag of wrapped candies.)

Say: **God appreciates everyone. If we learn to appreciate each other, we'll be able to show God's love to others just as Peter did to Cornelius. Instead of seeing our differences, we can look for important things to appreciate in each other. Let's make "appreciation sacks" to remind us that we can love what's inside of others, like God does. Choose someone you appreciate to work with. Decorate your bag with different animals to remind you of Peter's dream**

and how he learned to appreciate the differences in Cornelius.

Hand each child a paper sack. Set out markers and encourage children to decorate their sacks. As they work, circulate and make such comments as "I appreciate how well you work together" or "I appreciate all the creativity I see here today!"

After three or four minutes, tell the children to put away the markers. Say: **All of your appreciation sacks are beautiful! I really appreciate your talents and gifts.**

Hand each child three pieces of the wrapped candy, then say: **You each have three candies. Every time I clap my hands, find a partner and tell one thing you appreciate about him or her. Then drop a piece of candy in his or her appreciation sack.**

When everyone's been affirmed three times, say: **It's important to say what we appreciate about each other. Though we may be different in some ways, we can all spread God's love.**

6. Many Yet One

(You'll need a Bible, a sheet of poster board, cellophane tape, and markers. Before this activity, draw a large circle on the poster board and cut it out. Then cut the circle into puzzle pieces so each child has one.)

Have children find a place to work. Hold up the Bible and say: **God wants us to appreciate and accept all people. We're not so different. In fact, the Bible tells us we're really one! Let's see what the Bible says about being one.**

Open to Galatians 3:28b and read it aloud. Say: **God tells us we're one in Jesus. God tells us we're one in him. We're going to make a project to remind us how we may seem different**

but we're really one in God.

Hand each child a piece of the puzzle. Don't tell the children what the pieces will make when they're put together. Have them decorate their puzzle pieces as they wish and write their names across the center of the pieces.

When everyone's finished, work together to construct the circle puzzle on the wall in your classroom or hallway. Help the children tape each piece in place. Add Galatians 3:28b as a caption.

Say: **Look at this beautiful circle. It shows we're part of God's circle of endless love. We're all different, yet God wants us to appreciate each other just as we are. Be sure to take home your appreciation sacks and remember how much you're appreciated and loved!**

by Christine Yount

18. God Makes Us New (Paul)

The idea of becoming a "new person" is hard for children to understand. They see the world in a literal sense. Yet even children as young as 5 know the difference between old and new, and shiny and dull. The story of Paul on the road to Damascus is a good lesson to help children see the difference between a heart that's dull and a heart that's been made like new.

Use this lesson to help children see how God's love inside their hearts can shine out to touch other people.

A POWERFUL POINT

God can make his love shine through us.

A LOOK AT THE LESSON

1. A Polishing Touch (9 minutes)
2. A Bright Light (8 minutes)
3. The Road to Damascus (7 minutes)
4. Love Shines Through (9 minutes)
5. A Penny for Your Thoughts (8 minutes)
6. Concentration (5 minutes)

A SPRINKLING OF SUPPLIES

Gather a Bible, baking soda, a bowl, several pieces of dull silverware, rags, newspapers, a flashlight, salt, vinegar, a dirty penny for each child, and a small glass jar. You'll also need a heart-shaped cookie-cutter, bread, bologna, square slices of cheese, and napkins.

THE FUN-TO-LEARN LESSON

1. A Polishing Touch

(You'll need rags, newspapers, baking soda, a bowl, water, and several dull pieces of silverware. Before this activity, mix baking soda and water together in a bowl until they're the consistency of paste.)

Seat children on the floor with you. Hold up a spoon. Ask:

● **How do you suppose this spoon became so dirty and dull?**

● **Is there a way to make it look new again?**

Have children each find a partner. Spread newspapers on the work area. Set out rags and the bowl of baking soda paste. Let each pair of kids shine a fork or spoon.

When the silverware is shiny, set aside the polishing materials. Have children join you in a circle on the floor and ask:

● **How are the spoons and forks different now from when you first saw them?**

Say: **The difference in this silverware is that it looks shiny and like new. The polish you rubbed onto the forks and spoons helped them look shiny and new. That's how it is with God's love. Once we have Jesus in our hearts and soak God's love into our lives, his love shines through us, and we become shiny and new. Today I'll share a story about a man who became like new with God's love.**

2. A Bright Light

(You'll need a Bible and a flashlight.)

Sit with the children in a circle on the floor. Open the Bible to Acts 9. Hold up the Bible and say: **The Bible story I'm going to share with you today is about someone who was made new by God. You can help me tell the story. We'll pass this flashlight around the circle. When I stop, the person with the flashlight may turn it on and shine it on him- or herself. Then that person can pass it on as I tell more of the story.**

Hand the flashlight to the child sitting next to you as you begin telling the story of Paul. Say: **Saul was a man who didn't love Jesus. He wanted to put the people who loved Jesus in jail.** (Stop and have the child holding the flashlight shine it on him- or herself.)

Saul was on his way to a town called Damascus. He was going to Damascus to arrest anyone who loved Jesus. (Stop.) **As Saul walked along the road, a bright light from heaven flashed around him, and Saul fell to the ground!** (Stop.) **Then Saul heard a voice say, "Saul, Saul, why are you hurting me?" And Saul asked, "Who are you, Lord?" The voice said, "I am Jesus."** (Stop.)

Jesus said, "I am Jesus, the one you're hurting. Get up and go to the city of Damascus. Someone there will tell you what you must do." (Stop.)

Saul stood up to leave. He opened his eyes, but he couldn't see—Saul was blind! (Stop.) **Saul's friends had heard the voice speaking to Saul, but they hadn't seen anyone there. Saul's friends took his hands and led him to the city of Damascus. For three days, Saul couldn't see, and he didn't eat or drink.** (Stop.)

Jesus told Ananias to go see Saul. Jesus wanted Saul to do important work and shine with God's love. (Stop.) **So Ananias went to Saul. When Ananias laid his hands upon Saul, something like fish scales fell from Saul's eyes, and he could see again! God gave Saul back his sight!** (Stop.) **Saul loved Jesus and wanted to work hard for Jesus. God's love was shining out from Saul. Once Saul's heart was dull, but God made Saul's heart shiny and new! God's love could now shine through Saul.**

Be sure each child has had a turn to shine the flashlight. Then ask:

● **Why was Saul so mean to God's people?** (Guide children to see that it was because Saul didn't understand that Jesus is God's Son.)

● **How do you think Saul felt when the bright light blinded him and Jesus spoke to him?**

● **How was Saul different by the end of the story?**

Tell the kids that Saul is also known as Paul. Shine the flashlight back and forth around the circle and say: **When God called Paul to love him, Paul said yes to God. When God's love shines inside us, we can let God's love shine on the outside, too. God wants us to let his love shine out to others.**

3. The Road to Damascus

Say: **Let's sing about Paul walking on the road to Damascus.**

Lead children in singing "The Road to Damascus," sung to the tune of "The Battle Hymn of the Republic." Do the motions with the song.

"THE ROAD TO DAMASCUS"

God spoke one day to Paul as he was walking down the road,
(walk in place)

left, right, left, right, Paul walked along the road.
(Step to the left, step to the right.)
God spoke one day to Paul as he was walking down the road,
(walk in place)
and Paul said YES to God.
(Raise arms in the air and shout "Yes!")
Optional chorus:
 Glory, glory hallelujah,
 Glory, glory hallelujah,
 (hold arms and hands over head and sway)
 Glory, glory hallelujah,
 (repeat above motion)
 Paul said YES to God.
(Shout "Yes!" and raise fist in the air.)

Try these other verses. If there's time, allow children to make up their own.

● "God spoke one day to Paul through a bright and shining light..."

● "God spoke one day to Paul because he wanted Paul to shine..."

● "God spoke one day to Paul to change his heart from dull to new..."

4. Love Shines Through

(You'll need a heart-shaped cookie-cutter, bread, bologna, square cheese slices, and napkins.

Before this activity, cut bread, bologna, and cheese so that each child receives a half slice of each. If you're using a large heart-shaped cookie-cutter, you may wish to use whole pieces of bread, bologna, and cheese.)

Gather children around a table. Say: **When we love God and obey him, God's love shines through us so others can see it.**

Ask:

● **How can we let God's love**

shine through us? (Answers may include by sharing with others, by loving all people, by showing forgiveness, and by helping others.)

Say: **Let's make a snack to remind us how God wants his love to shine through us.** Hand each child a napkin. Show them how to lay the cheese on top of the bread. Then let them use the cookie-cutter to cut a heart shape from the bologna. Lay the piece of bologna with the heart cut out on top of the cheese. Point out how the heart "shines through."

5. A Penny for Your Thoughts

(You'll need a dirty penny for each child, salt, vinegar, and a small jar.)

Give each child a dirty penny. Talk about how it looks dull and old. Ask:

● **How is this dirty, dull penny like Paul's heart before he met Jesus?** (Guide kids to see that Paul's heart was cold and dull because he was mean to others.)

● **How did Paul become like a new person?**

Say: **Let's see if we can help these pennies become shiny again.**

Mix ¼ cup vinegar and 1 teaspoon salt in the jar. Mix the salt and vinegar well. Have each child drop his or her penny into the jar. Let the children take turns gently shaking the jar. After a minute or two, lift out the pennies one at a time. Polish them with napkins or paper towels. Ask:

● **How are the pennies different from when we dropped them in the jar?**

● **We can make pennies shiny again, but who's the only one who can make a person shiny and like new again?**

Say: **God is the only one who can make our hearts shiny and our lives like new again. When we're made new by accepting Jesus, God's love shines through us.**

6. Concentration

Say: **In our story today, God made Paul blind for three days. During this time, Paul must have thought hard about all God was saying to him. When we think hard about something, we're concentrating. Closing our eyes when we pray helps us concentrate on listening to God. Let's close our eyes.** Allow a few moments of quiet.

Then pray: **Dear God, we thank you for your love. Please show us ways to let your love shine out to other people. Amen.**

Hand each child a shiny penny as he or she is leaving. Say: **This shiny penny will help you remember that God's love shines through us when we're made shiny and new in him.**

by Vicki Shannon

19. Fellow Friends (Barnabas)

From early childhood, children are told to be friendly and kind to others. For some children this comes easily, but for others it may be a constant effort. Children don't always recognize that friendliness is a condition of the heart. Kids need to see how acting helpful and friendly to others can become a positive, rewarding habit.

The story of Barnabas and Paul is a good illustration of the positive effects of being helpful and friendly. If Barnabas hadn't befriended Paul, Paul may not have become a great preacher of God's Word. So it is with kindness. We never know how our kind actions may affect someone in a positive way. Use this lesson to help children learn that God wants them to be helpful and friendly to others all the time.

A POWERFUL POINT

God wants us to be friendly and helpful to others.

A LOOK AT THE LESSON

1. Flower Power (8 minutes)
2. Friendly Surprise (8 minutes)
3. Help a Friend (6 minutes)
4. Planting Seeds (9 minutes)
5. Kindness Springs From My Heart (8 minutes)
6. Pop Out a Smile (9 minutes)

A SPRINKLING OF SUPPLIES

You'll need a Bible; two fresh flowers; a cup of water; yarn; a bag of small, wrapped candies; bean seeds; potting soil; markers; paper cups; red construction paper; scissors; cellophane tape; an old sheet, napkins, popcorn; and a popcorn popper.

THE FUN-TO-LEARN LESSON

1. Flower Power

(You'll need two fresh flowers and a cup of water. Fresh daisies work very well for this activity, but any flowers with lots of petals will work.)

Seat children with you in a circle on the floor. Set the cup of water in the center of the circle. Hold up one of the flowers and say: **We'll pass this flower around the circle. Say something mean and unfriendly to it as you pull off a petal.**

Continue until there are no petals left on the flower. Ask:

● **How is this like the way we sometimes treat people?**

Say: **Sometimes we say or do things that aren't friendly. We usually know right away when we've hurt someone's feelings. Let's pass another flower. This time say something kind to the flower. Be friendly—you may even sprinkle a little water on it if you'd like.**

After the flower has been passed to each child, ask:

● **If you water a flower and treat it kindly, can you see it grow right away?**

● **If you're helpful or friendly to someone, will you always see how they're feeling right away? Explain.**

Say: **Just because we don't always see the results of kind actions right away, that doesn't mean we aren't helping. God doesn't want to us to stop being friendly to others. God wants us to be helpful and friendly all the time. Today we'll learn about a man whose kindness helped lots of people learn about God.**

2. Friendly Surprise

(You'll need a Bible; yarn; red construction paper; and a bag of small, wrapped candies.

Before this activity, you'll need to make a "surprise ball." Begin by cutting a small heart from the red construction paper. Wrap yarn around and around the tiny paper heart until you've made a ball at least 3 inches across.)

Have kids sit with you on the floor. Open the Bible to Acts 9. Hold up the Bible and say: **Today's Bible story is about a man named Barnabas. Without his kindness, Paul may not have met the apostles and become a great preacher for God. You can help me tell the story. We'll pass this ball around the circle as I tell parts of the story. When I stop, the person holding the ball may unwind a little of the yarn as he or she retells the part of the story I just told.**

Begin passing the ball and say: **Paul had acted mean to people who loved Jesus. He'd put in jail many people who loved Jesus.** (Stop and have the child holding the yarn ball retell the first

two sentences of the story in his or her own words. Let the child unwind a portion of yarn. Then continue passing the ball.)

Even after Paul came to love Jesus, everyone was afraid of Paul. They didn't know if he really loved Jesus or if he was playing a mean trick. (Stop.) **Paul wanted to meet the apostles—Jesus' friends. But even the apostles were afraid of Paul and thought he might toss them in jail.** (Stop.) **One of Jesus' followers was named Barnabas. Barnabas was a kind man, and he took Paul to meet the apostles.** (Stop.)

Barnabas stood up for Paul. He told the apostles that Paul had changed and that he loved Jesus now. (Stop.) **Barnabas didn't know that God had a mighty plan for Paul. Barnabas just wanted to be kind and friendly.** (Stop.)

Before long, the apostles became friends with Paul. And Paul started to teach other people about Jesus' love. (Stop.) **Soon Paul was traveling all over the world telling people about Jesus. Paul was bringing good news about Jesus to thousands of God's people.** (Stop.)

Because Barnabas had been helpful and friendly to Paul, Paul was able to do God's work. (Stop.)

Have the child now holding the yarn ball retell the last sentence and unwind another small portion of the yarn. Have him or her hold the ball for a moment. Ask:

● **Why do you suppose Barnabas was friendly and helpful to Paul?**

● **Do you think Barnabas knew right away that Paul would be such a great man of God?**

Say: **We can't always see right away how being friendly will help some-**

one. **We can be helpful and friendly and then trust God to bring results.**

If any children haven't had a turn, let them finish unwinding the surprise ball. Then hold up the tiny heart and say: **Even though we can't always see how much our friendliness does, we know it reaches to the heart of that person. Just like this ball, sometimes there's a nice surprise when we're friendly and helpful—people will be friendly and helpful to us!** Hand each child a piece of wrapped candy to enjoy.

3. Help a Friend

Have children form pairs. If there's an uneven number of kids, choose one child to be "It" before you pair children up. If there's an even number of children, join the game yourself.

Say: **We're going to play a game to learn about helpful friends. With your partner, choose who'll be the Friend and who'll be the Helper.** Pause for kids to decide. **The Friends will stand at one end of the room. They're stuck there until the Helpers come to help them home. The Helpers will be at the opposite end of the room. We'll have It stand in the center. When I say "go," the Helpers will try to get to their Friends and touch them without getting tagged by It. If the Helpers reach their Friends, the two may walk back across the room together and not be tagged. If a Helper gets tagged while trying to reach his or her partner, both the Helper and that Friend are out until next game.**

Play the game a few times, switching roles. Then gather the kids in a circle on the floor. Ask:

● **When is a time a friend helped you?**

● **Why do you think it's a good idea to be kind and helpful?**

Say: **Just as Barnabas was loving and kind to Paul, we can spread God's love by being helpful and kind to other people.**

4. Planting Seeds

(You'll need markers, bean seeds, potting soil, and a paper cup for each child.)

Gather kids around a table and say: **God wants us to be helpful and friendly to others. When we're kind, we plant the seeds of love in someone's heart, just like Barnabas helped plant the seeds of God's love in Paul's heart. Let's plant some seeds to remind us that being helpful and friendly can show God's love.**

Show the kids how to plant bean seeds in paper cups. If time allows, let them decorate the cups with markers. When you're finished, ask:

● **What will happen if you water the seeds and give them sun?**

● **How is giving water and sun to the seeds like being kind to them?**

● **How is this like being kind to other people?**

Say: **We may not always know how that friendliness and help affects other people, but we do know we're spreading God's love. When we're helpful and friendly, love springs up and grows like God's flowers. As you water your seeds and care for them, remember to plant the seeds of kindness by being friendly and helpful to others.**

5. Kindness Springs From My Heart

(You'll need red construction paper, scissors, cellophane tape, and markers. Before class, cut a 1×5-inch strip of paper for each child.)

Hand each child a piece of red construction paper and one construction paper strip. Have kids cut a heart from the piece of red construction paper. Tell children to draw on the heart something helpful or kind that they could do for another person. Demonstrate how to accordion-fold the paper strip. Tape the end of the folded strip to the heart. When the heart is pushed down, it will spring back up.

After everyone's finished, sit with the children in a circle on the floor. Have them hold the hearts they made. Say: **God wants us to look for ways we can be helpful and friendly to others.**

Ask:

● **Who can tell about a time he or she acted friendly or helpful to another person?**

● **How did you feel when you acted this way?**

● **Why is it important to be friendly to everyone and not just the people we like?**

Say: **I'll choose someone to walk over to another person in the circle. You'll say, "Friendliness springs from my heart. I'll be a friend to you!" Then hand the person you walked over to the heart you made and sit in his or her place. He or she may then choose a person to walk over to.**

Continue until everyone has a heart and has been affirmed.

6. Pop Out a Smile

(You'll need an old sheet, napkins, popcorn, and a popcorn popper. Before this activity, be sure your popcorn popper has a cord long enough to reach the floor. You may need to use a heavy extension cord.)

Spread an old sheet on the floor. Set the popcorn popper in the center of the sheet. Sit with kids around the edge. Say: **We've been learning that being helpful and friendly is God's way. When we're helpful and friendly, God's love pops out all over!**

Let's make a popcorn snack. When you see or hear a kernel of corn pop, jump up and pop out the name of someone who's friendly, helpful, or kind. It may be someone in your family, one of your friends, or someone in this room.

When the popcorn's finished popping, set the popper out of reach of the children. Hand each child a napkin. Let them each take a handful of popcorn to eat. Say: **It was fun to hear you pop out such friendly words and names! Let's say a prayer asking God to help us be friendly, helpful people. Dear God, please be with us this week as we try to be friendly and helpful. Help us be kind even when people aren't kind to us. May kindness pop from our hearts to everyone around us. Amen.**

by Sheila Halasz

20. Smile 'n' Serve! (Paul's Helpers)

Paul was known as the "great servant of God." He chose to serve God and help others in all he did. Paul had many helpers in his service to God—Priscilla, Aquila, Timothy, Gaius, and many more were all willing and eager to serve God through serving others. Their work wasn't always easy and certainly wasn't glamorous. But through their love and help, many people came to know Jesus.

Young children are natural helpers. They know how good it feels to see a smile of thanks on someone's face or feel a pat on the back for their help. Children need to learn that God wants them to serve others even when it's hard because when they serve others, they're serving God, too.

A POWERFUL POINT

Serving and helping others makes us feel great!

A LOOK AT THE LESSON

1. Start Servin' (8 minutes)
2. The Name Game (9 minutes)
3. Your Serve! (6 minutes)
4. Servin' Sandwiches (9 minutes)
5. Serve the Lord (8 minutes)
6. Give 'Em a Hand (7 minutes)

A SPRINKLING OF SUPPLIES

Gather a Bible, paper cups, plastic spoons, a pitcher of lemonade, eight balloons, a permanent marker, crackers, three apples, raisins, cinnamon, a cheese grater, a bowl, mixing spoons, and napkins.

THE FUN-TO-LEARN LESSON

1. Start Servin'

(You'll need a Bible, a paper cup and plastic spoon for each child, and a pitcher of lemonade.)

Put children in pairs. Say: **Today we're going to learn about what it means to serve one another and to serve God. We'll begin by giving you a chance to serve your partner.** Give one child in each pair a half cup of lemonade. Make sure all the cups have equal amounts of lemonade. Hand the other child in each pair a plastic spoon.

Say: **When I say, "Start serving," the partner with the spoon will begin serving his or her partner by spooning lemonade into the partner's mouth. When you've emptied the cup, the person who drank the lemonade says, "Thanks for serving!" Then partners can switch places and we'll play the game again.**

Give clean cups and spoons to pairs as they switch roles. After each child has had a chance to serve and be served, ask:

● **Was it hard to serve your partner? Why or why not?**

● **How did you feel being served?**

Say: **God wants us to serve others with a helpful heart. Even when it's hard to serve someone, God wants us to do our best. When we help and serve other people, it makes us feel good, and it's a way to share God's love with others. Our Bible story today is about how some men and women helped and served others as they shared God's love.**

2. The Name Game

(You'll need a Bible, eight balloons, and a permanent marker.

Before this activity, blow up and tie off eight balloons. With a permanent marker, write the following names on separate balloons: Priscilla, Aquila, Andronicus, Junia, Gaius, Timothy, Epaphroditus, and Onesiphorus. For extra fun, add a smiley face on one side of each balloon. Also, mark the following passages in your Bible: Romans 16:3, 7, 23; Philippians 2:19-30; Colossians 4:7-15; and 2 Timothy 1:16-18.)

Gather the children in a circle on the floor. Hold up the Bible. Point to it and say: **The Bible has many stories of friends helping each other. We also learn about serving each other in the Bible.**

Ask:

● **What does it mean to help someone?**

● **What does it mean to serve someone?**

● **How are helping and serving other people alike? different?**

● **Why do you think God wants us to help and serve others?**

Say: **Serving others is an important job. Our story is found in four books of the Bible: Romans, Philippians, Colossians, and 2 Timothy.**

We all know that God had a servant named Paul. Paul served God by telling lots of people about Jesus and Jesus' love. But Paul wasn't the only one who served God. Paul had many friends who helped him serve God by serving other people in special ways. Hold up a balloon. **I'm going to introduce each of Paul's servant friends to you, and I'll tell how they served. Then we'll pass the balloon, and you can repeat the names. They're fun names to say and learn.**

Hold up the Gaius (pronounced GAY-us) balloon and say: **This is Paul's friend Gaius. Gaius served people who loved Jesus by letting them use his home as a meeting place. Being friendly and making people welcome in your home is a way to serve God.** Pass the balloon and let children repeat Gaius' name aloud.

When the Gaius balloon has traveled back to you, pick up the Timothy balloon and say: **This is Paul's friend Timothy. Timothy served others with his kindness and by telling people about Jesus' love. Telling about Jesus is one way to serve God.** Pass the balloon and have each child say Timothy's name.

Hold up the Epaphroditus (pronounced ee-PAF-ro-DYE-tus) balloon and say: **This is Paul's friend Epaphroditus. Epaphroditus served other people even though he was sick. He told people all about Jesus and encouraged them to love Jesus, too. It doesn't matter if we're sick or well, we can serve God no matter what.** Pass the balloon and repeat Epaphroditus' name.

Pick up the Onesiphorus (pronounced OH-nih-SIF-uh-russ) balloon and say: **This is Paul's friend Onesiphorus. Onesiphorus helped serve Paul by being his friend. Onesiphorus was not ashamed that Paul had been in** jail. **Being a faithful friend is a good way to serve God.** Pass the balloon.

Introduce each of the next two sets of names as a pair. Hold up two balloons at once and say: **These are Paul's friends Andronicus** (pronounced an-DRON-i-cus) **and Junia** (pronounced JUNE-ee-ah). **Andronicus and Junia served faithfully with Paul while they were all in jail. They kept loving and telling people about Jesus. Being loyal even through hard times is a way to serve God.** Pass both balloons at once and have children repeat the names.

Hold up the last two balloons. Say: **These are Paul's friends Priscilla** (pronounced prih-SIL-uh) **and Aquila** (AK-wi-lah). **Priscilla and Aquila served other people by letting people safely stay in their house. Helping others by protecting them is a way to serve God.** Pass both balloons at once and let children say Priscilla's and Aquila's names.

When all the balloons have been passed, say: **Paul and his helpers brought a lot of happiness to the people they helped and served. Each friend helped in a different way. There are many ways to serve people, and they're not always easy. But when we serve and help others, we're serving God, too.**

3. Your Serve!

(You'll need the balloons from the previous activity.)

Have children stand with you in a circle and say: **Paul and his helpers served God by serving other people. Even when times were hard, they continued to serve. Paul's helpers didn't give up and let others down. Don't let them fall now!** Begin serving each balloon volleyball-style into the circle until all eight balloons are being bopped in the air. Encourage the children to keep the balloons from touching the ground. They may tap the balloons with their hands, bop them with their heads, or blow on them to keep them in the air.

After a minute or two, set the balloons aside and ask:

● **Do you think it's always easy to help and serve other people? Why or why not?**

● **Who can tell about a time he or she helped or served someone?**

Say: It's not always easy to help other people. **Sometimes we get busy and don't notice when others need our help. Or we may think we can't find a way to help them. God helps us find ways to serve people, and he doesn't want us to give up when the going gets tough. When we serve other people, we're doing as God desires. When we serve others, we're also serving God.**

4. Servin' Sandwiches

(You'll need crackers, three apples, ¼ cup raisins, 1 teaspoon cinnamon, a cheese grater, a large bowl, mixing spoons, and napkins.)

Have the children wash their hands. Gather them around a table. Set up an assembly line for preparing this unusual snack. Form the following groups: the graters, the sprinklers, the spicettes, the mixers, and the spooners.

The graters will be in charge of grating the apples—skins and all. Tell the graters to be very careful and to grate slowly so they don't cut themselves. Have the graters put the grated apple into a bowl.

The sprinklers will sprinkle raisins into a mixing bowl. The spicettes will add tiny dashes of cinnamon to the apples and raisins. The mixers will take turns mixing the ingredients in the bowl. And the spooners will spoon some of the filling onto crackers and put two crackers on each napkin.

While the children work, affirm their helping actions with comments such as "I like the way James helped pick up the spilled raisins" or "You're all such good helpers. Helping people is a way to serve them."

When you've made enough crackers for each child to have two, say: **This apple salad is like a food called haroset** (pronounced HAR-oh-set). **Haroset is a Jewish treat. This is the type of food Paul and his friends might have served each other for special dinners.**

Ask:

● **What are some ways to serve others? Think back to the Bible story about Paul's helpers and how they served people.** Responses may include by helping them, by being a faithful friend, by making people feel welcome in our homes, or by encouraging others.

● **Why do you think serving others pleases God?**

Say: **In Paul's time, people often sat on the ground when they ate. Find a partner and a place to sit together.** Allow time for children to pair up and get situated. **In Paul's time, people were served their meals by friends or members of their families. Let's see what it's like to serve our friends their snacks. Choose which of you will come first to get a napkin with crackers. Take the treat to your partner and set it in front of him or her. Then your partner will bring a napkin with crackers to you.**

As you enjoy your unusual snack, say: **It's not only important to help**

and serve others, but it's fun and makes us feel good, too! When we use our hands to serve, we're also using our hearts to serve God.**

5. Serve the Lord

Gather kids in a circle on the floor. Lead your children in singing "Serve the Lord" to the tune of "Bingo." The last time through, you'll be clapping the letters to the word "serve" instead of singing them. For young children, write the letters S, E, R, V, and E on the chalkboard or a sheet of paper for them to look at while singing and clapping. Point to each letter as it's sung or clapped.

"SERVE THE LORD"

Help and serve and don't be late, 'cause serving makes us feel great! S-E-R-V-E! S-E-R-V-E! S-E-R-V-E! I want to serve the Lord!

6. Give 'Em a Hand

Have the children sit in a circle on the floor. Say: **We've seen how Paul and his friends served other people. We've even helped and served each other. But...**

● **Who do we always want to serve first?**

● **What are some ways we can serve God?** (Guide children to say things like "through prayer," "by obeying God's Word," "by being kind to others," or "by being honest.")

Say: **In all we do and say, we want to serve God first. When we serve God first, we can use our hands and hearts to serve others.**

Hold out your hand to a child and say: **I can serve God by praying. And I can help you, too.** Help the child stand up. Then that child will offer his or her hand to the next child and tell a way he or she can serve God. Children might choose ways such as reading the Bible or helping others.

When everyone is standing, join hands and say: **Serving and helping others is a good way to spread God's love. Let's close with a prayer asking God to help us find ways to serve others. Dear Lord, help us be like Paul and his helpers who served you by serving others. Please help us find ways we may help other people and spread your love to them. Amen.**

Say: **Let's keep looking for ways to help and serve others with God's love every day this week. Serving others makes us feel great!**

by Nanette Goings

Teacher Notes

Teacher Notes

Teacher Notes

Teacher Notes